The Spice of Life

SICHUAN

by Samantha Wilson and Scott Lewis

Matric International Publishing House

Copyright

ISBN 978-0-9809476-1-8

Please help us keep this guide up to date

As China continues its headlong rush into modernisation, nothing stays the same for very long. We've done our best to ensure that information contained in the guide is accurate, monitoring changes and making last-minute updates right up to the time of press, but we would be delighted to hear from travelers about further changes or suggested improvements to the guide. Those making the most helpful contributions will receive a copy of the Sichuan, the Spice of Life of their choice. Please write to us at the following address.

Matric International Publishing House (迈萃国际出版)

China (中国)
Senior Partner：Quan Xinying
TEL：+86) 10 8576 9542
ADD：Rm41-9-301, No. 29 Jianguo Rd,
　　 Chaoyang District, Beijing,
　　 100025 China
Web: www.cnlookingglass.com

Canada (加拿大)
Senior Partner: Royston Tester
TEL：001 416 712 5157
ADD：369, Manning Avenue,
　　 Toronto, Ontario,
　　 Canada, M6G 2V6
Email: bjmatric@163.com

Tourism Administration of Sichuan Province (四川省旅游局)
TEL：+86) 28 8667 0508
ADD：65, Section 2, Renmingnan Rd, Chengdu, Sichuan, China
Web：www.scta.gov.cn

Acknowledgements

We would just like to say a big thank you to several people without whom this book wouldn't have been possible. Firstly, thanks to everyone at the Sichuan Tourism board for all their help and support, particularly Zhang Gu, Jenny Zhou and Cheng Guofan. Thanks also go to Dan, Emily, Chris and everyone else at Chengdu Pandas Rugby Club for showing us around the town and being wonderful company. To Yonatan Bental we'd like to say thanks so much for pointing us in the right direction and for his endless knowledge of Sichuan. Thanks also to Liu Hong for his advice and translation help, Sarah Trott for her meticulous editing and to Monique Jansen and Ray Au for their beautiful photographs.

This book would never have happened without the help of Michelle Ming, our wonderful translator who never stopped smiling and who kept our spirits up when times got tough, and to Shyoki Zhou, who helped two manic writers go from a series of Word documents to the book you now hold.

Thanks of course to our families and friends for all their encouragement, support and advice during the writing of this book. Lastly, we would like to dedicate this book to Fiona Lee and Niv Silberman, for putting up with us and all the associated stress that comes from living with freelance writers.

Samantha Wilson and Scott Lewis,

《外国人看四川》序言

四川省旅游局局长 张谷

　　四川拥有极为丰富的旅游资源,拥有众多高品位的自然景观和人文景观。全省现有4000多处旅游景区景点,其中世界级、国家级和省级以上旅游景区(点)900多个,世界自然和文化遗产5处,是中国拥有世界遗产最多的省份,也是中国唯一拥有世界自然遗产、文化遗产、自然与文化双遗产的省份。四川也是中国历史深厚、文化璀璨的地区,三星堆、金沙遗址的发掘,说明了长江流域文化在中华文明史上占据着重要的位置。作为中国第二大藏族聚居区、最大的彝族聚居区和唯一的羌族聚居区的四川,丰富的民族文化、多彩的民俗和众多高品位的自然景观,相互交融,构筑了四川得天独厚的旅游资源。此外,冰雪、温泉、古镇、美食也是四川具有代表性的旅游资源,充满了引人入胜的魅力。很多旅游者都有这样的体会:四川,是一个来了还想再来的地方。

　　古人云:天下山水之观在蜀。此外,世界上85%的大熊猫生活在四川,故四川被誉为大熊猫的故乡,她以美丽动人的自然风光,悠久灿烂的历史文化,绚丽多姿的民俗风情,成为中国西部一道独特的风景,希望每位读者都能在本书中发现自己喜爱的目的地,热情好客的四川人民,期待着世界各地朋友到熊猫故乡－－四川来旅游观光。请您记住:天下四川,熊猫故乡。

Preface

Mr Zhang Gu, President of Sichuan Tourism Bureau

Sichuan is a province full of tourism opportunities, with breathtaking natural landscapes sheltering a range of exciting cultural experiences. With over 4,000 unique tourist attractions – including over 900 world-class, state-level or provincial-level beauty spots and five World Heritage sites – Sichuan is recognised the world over as one of China's most beautiful and culturally diverse provinces.

Sichuan is a province with a rich, splendid cultural history. The ruins at Sanxingdui and Jinsha tell us just how important the Yangtze river basin was to the development of early Chinese civilisation, while modern Sichuan is home to the second largest Tibetan population in China, the biggest Yi minority group, and China's only ethnic Qiang community.

From the snowy, icy peaks of Gongga Shan to the grasslands of Tagong,and the ancient walled town of Songpan to the hot springs of Hailuguo, Sichuan has something to offer everyone. Our cuisine is famous throughout the world, and adds to the province's charm and individuality. There is an old saying in Sichuan: "When someone visits, he will not want to leave." We are sure that many of our tourists feel the same.

85% of the world's Giant Pandas live and breed in Sichuan, giving our province the nickname "Home of the Giant Panda." This, combined with our beautiful natural scenery, long history and plethora of ethnic traditions and culture, makes Sichuan province a unique region in the west of China.

We hope every reader of this book can find something to love here in Sichuan. We welcome our friends from all over the world to Sichuan and hope that, like the old saying, you too will find yourself unwilling to leave.

Sichuan's rich, fertile soils have long since awarded it the title 'The Land of Abundance', a name perfectly befitting a region that exudes abundance in every possible way. Colourful ethnic minorities from every corner of the country have found their place in the province, their traditions, age-old cultures and sheer diversity adorning the dramatic landscape. From the inhospitable and alluring snow-capped peaks that tumble in from Tibet, to the vast, sweeping plains of the Sichuan Basin, the province leaves not a single geographical marvel unrepresented.

Home to great Chinese politicians and poets, it was on these lands that illustrious and histrionic battles played out, where ancient civilisations evolved and where events took place that changed the face of China.

Both modern and traditional, Sichuan has retained its cultural and natural heritage whilst moving into the 21st century with force. Home to five UNESCO desig-nated sites it is also leading the world in the battle to save the Giant Panda, an animal that has become not just the symbol of Sichuan, but of the entire country.

From its eclectic mix of people to its world famous spicy cuisine, from its lakes and waterfalls to its gla-ciers and grasslands and from its poignant past to its protected pandas, Sichuan is most undoubtedly 'The Land of Abundance'.

Sichuan and it's Prefectures

Contents

Introducing Sichuan

Practicalities

The Guide

INTRODUCING SICHUAN

The Story So Far

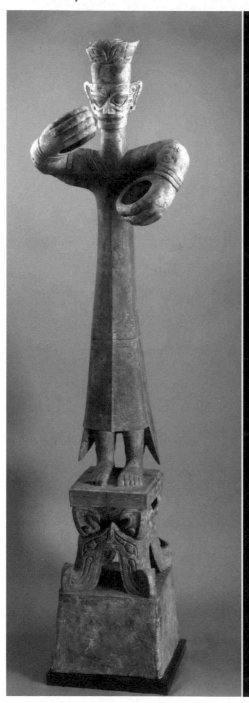

Sichuan has certainly had one of the more turbulent histories amongst the Chinese provinces, being home to indignant independent kingdoms, the staging ground for countless revolutions, and continuously challenging the authority of those who seek to conquer or subjugate it.

Considered a simple, primitive, backwater province, at least until the Qin empire came along and (after a series of very bloody campaigns) pacified the region in the 3rd century BC, Sichuan had very little to offer historians. The remains of the Baodun people, a Neolithic tribe known for decorating the walls of their houses with pebbles, had been discovered at several sites on the Sichuan basin and dated as far back as 2,500BC, but no advanced culture had been found on the plains.

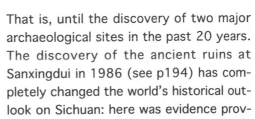

That is, until the discovery of two major archaeological sites in the past 20 years. The discovery of the ancient ruins at Sanxingdui in 1986 (see p194) has completely changed the world's historical outlook on Sichuan: here was evidence proving without a shadow of a doubt that some hitherto unknown and highly advanced civilisation made its home on the Chengdu plain some 3,500 years ago.

Then, in 2001, the discovery of a second site at Jinsha (see p200) provided evidence that this civilisation, named the Ancient Shu, inhabited the central part of Sichuan until at least midway through the Western Zhou Dynasty.

The Shu and the Ba

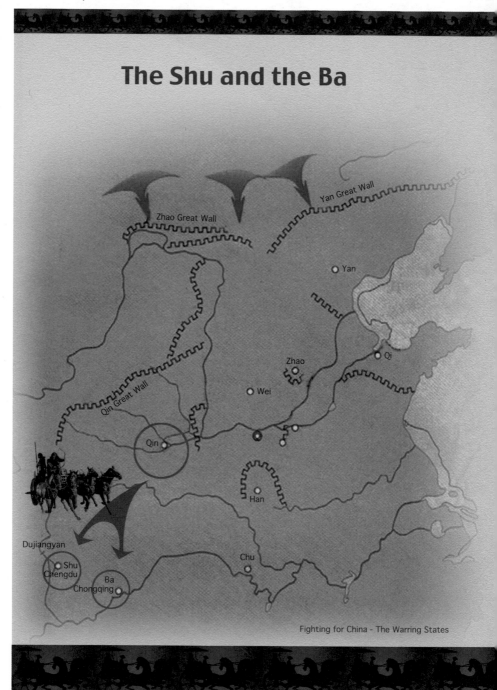

Fighting for China - The Warring States

During the Warring States Period, the kingdom of Ancient Shu had a direct competitor – to the southeast, the kingdom of Ba fanned out from its capital city in Zhi (roughly the site of modern-day Chongqing), spreading westward onto the Chengdu Plain. Mostly fishermen and hunters, the Ba were a loose confederation of tribes and clans, ruled by a single king to which all others paid tribute. They were famous warriors, and many Ba soldiers served as mercenaries in the armies of the other states.

When the neighbouring kingdom of Qin decided to invade Shu, Ba sided with the Qin and their allies, quickly subjugating and destroying the Ancient Shu. To show their gratitude, the Qin promptly attacked the weakened Ba, bringing the whole of Sichuan into the Qin empire. The two kingdoms were allowed to keep their own leaders – the kings were given a title similar to that of marquis in Western history – but were kept oppressed by strict military rule and a strict integration program imposed by the Qin.

Of course, the Shu and Ba refused to roll over and accept the new order, and so the people of the two kingdoms led hundreds of revolutions against the Qin and their new emperor, King Huiwen. When Huiwen died in 310 BC, the entire state rose up in rebellion led, oddly, by one of the Qin's ministers, a Shu by the name of Chen Zhuang. This rebellion was swiftly crushed, as were two more led by descendants of the rulers of Ancient Shu. After the second, led by Marquis Wan, the Qin governor of Shu, Zhang Ruo, removed the royal families from power. Increasing numbers of soldiers were used to beat the people of Ba and Shu into submission, and the province was finally pacified, integrated into the Qin Empire completely, and eventually used as a dumping ground for any poor soul sent into exile.

Life under the Qin

And so the kingdoms of Shu and Ba fell into obscurity. Yet even as their glory was fading, the next major step in Sichuan's evolution was about to be taken. Governor Li Bing, seeing the damage wrought by the annual flooding of the mighty Min River, ordered the construction of the Dujiangyuan Irrigation Project (see p186), bringing the flooding to an end and irrigating vast tracts of the Sichuan Basin that had previously been untenable for farming.

In the shadow of this massive-scale project, a small settlement began to grow. Originally a home for those working on the project, farmers and tradesmen soon flocked to this new city, straddling the Jinjiang rivers. This rapidly growing settlement was named the 'Perfect City'- or Chengdu.

Li Bing

Li Bing's project enabled the Qin's empire to become bigger, richer, and more powerful than any of the previous kingdoms. But it didn't save the rulers from internal strife, and in 210 BC Emperor Qin Shi Huang died of natural causes, leaving only an incompetent son who was controlled utterly by corrupt ministers in the Qin courts.

Qin Shi Huang

Within three years, there were widespread uprisings from the poor, often led by descendents of the Shu and Ba peoples. After the dust from these uprisings settled, the country was split into 19 city states, which then spent the next five years warring amongst themselves. Eventually, the state of Han (consisting of what is now modern Sichuan, Chongqin, and southern Shaanxi) and its ruler, Liu Bang, came to power.

Liu Bang

The Three Kingdoms Period

Under the Han, China had over 400 years of turbulent but productive rule. Great advances were made in engineering, craftsmanship, and naturally, warfare. Taoism and Confucianism both waxed and waned in popularity during this period. North of Sichuan, the Silk Road opened up trade to parts of the West, reaching as far as the Roman Empire.

China began to slowly develop a system similar to feudalism in the West, whereby peasants would pledge their loyalty to landholders, who would in turn (supposedly) owe allegiance to the crown. One of these landowners eventually usurped power for themselves, creating the short-lived Xin Dynasty, but once again rebellion and warfare put the Han back in charge.

The Han was never the most stable regime, and some two hundred years after the dynasty was back in power plotting and intrigue led to the break-up of the Empire. After years of intrigue and conflict, Emperor Xian was taken hostage by the warlord Cao Cao. The events leading up to Cao Cao's rise to power are exceptionally complex, and far beyond the scope of this book. However, they are recorded in the first part of the *Three Kingdoms Romance,* for a more comprehensive look into this time.

For now, it is enough to know that after Cao Cao's usurpation of the throne, China broke up into three large kingdoms: Cao Cao's son, Cao Pi, forced the Emperor to abdicate and set up the state of Wei in the north, Sun Quan was named king of Wu, in the south-east, while in the area around modern day Sichuan, a distant relative of Emperor Xian named Liu Bei, a former loyalist general and master strategist, set up the kingdom of Shu-Han.

The three states launched into an endless tête-a-tête, making and breaking alliances at the drop of a feather. After the death of Liu Bei at the Battle of Yiling, the three states forced each other into an impasse despite military successes by Shu-Han forces under the direction of Zhuge Liang. After Liang's death in 234 AD, the politics of the Shu-Hans became controlled by corrupt eunuchs and councilors, and in 263 Wei launched a final decisive strike against the weakened kingdom, capturing Chengdu and forcing Emperor Liu Shan to surrender.

This marked the end of the Three Kingdoms period and shortly after this the Cao family was replaced by the Sima family as heads of the Wei kingdom. It was not long before the kingdom of Wu was conquered by the much larger Wei, providing the basis for dynastic rule all the way through to 1911.

Zhuge Liang

Rise of the Republic

Even though Sichuan continued to be a hotbed of discontent and rebellion throughout the next 1500 years, it slowly became more and more assimilated into what we now know as China. Art and poetry, not warfare, became the pursuits the people of the Chengdu plains were known for. Religious thought was encouraged and many famous Taoist and Buddhist scholars lived in the regions around Mount Emei and Mount Qingcheng.

Sichuan entered something of a golden age, as many of the artistic and cultural traditions that the province is famed for developed around this time. Temples, palaces, and gardens sprung up everywhere. Massive developments in agriculture helped keep the province at the centre of trade across the country.

Although the strife between the Ming and Qing dynasties almost decimated Sichuan – some say that 75% of the population was killed due to battle, starvation and disease- the province recovered and flourished during the 16th and 17th centuries. Rapid construction during the 18th and 19th century meant that, by the turn of the 20th century, the province was linked to the main Chinese railroad network by the Yuehan and Chuanhan railways.

However, throughout China's provinces, people were also dissatisfied with Imperial rule. Intellectuals, educated in the West and impressed with the systems of democracy that had long since replaced the monarchies, called for power to be handed down to the people.

Naturally, the Qing regime, under the figurehead of Emperor Puyi (but in reality ruled by the Emperor's ministers) tried everything they could to put down this revolutionary method of thinking, and eventually they went too far.

After the events that centred around the 1911 Sichuan Railway Protection Movement (see p152), China erupted into civil unrest. Chengdu was besieged by the rebels, and troops from Hubei Province were sent in to Sichuan by the terrified Qing Government to quell the rebellion. This left Hubei undefended, and the populace there rose up in what is now termed the Wuchang Uprising – the action that officially marked the start of the overthrow of the Qing and the foundation of the Provisional Republic of China.

Sun Yat Sen

The Long March

The Republic, under Sun Yat Sen, brought a short period of respite from the conflicts and uprisings. It was not to last though, as after Sun's death in 1925, the Republic split into two parties. One was the Guomindang, or Nationalist Party that was led by the man many saw as Sun Yat Sen's heir-apparent, Chiang Kai-shek (the Westernised form of his Chinese name, Jiang Jieshi). The other was the Communist Party of China, which had only come into formal existence a few years previously.

It was around this time that a man named Mao Zedong rose to prominence amidst the Communist ranks. At this point, the Communists were the target of a massive extermination campaign by the Guomindang, but their army and following continued to grow. By 1930, some 42,000 soldiers made up the bulk of the Communist army, and they began to offer resistance against the Nationalists.

By 1934, the tide of battle was going strongly against Mao and his Comrades. A series of military movements from Communist leaders ignoring Mao's authority led to the First Red Army being trapped in Jiangxi Province. As the Nationalists tightened their grip, the Communist leadership saw one way out; a breakout and relocation to Shaanxi, 13,000km away.

Mao Zhedong

This dramatic undertaking has since become known as the Long March, an epic trek across five provinces, over mountains and through treacherous weather. Over 90,000 Communists started the march along with Mao and his fellow leaders. Only 20,000 made it to the other side.

Several of the major battles of the Long March took place in Sichuan, and the province is littered with sites where the Communists faced trials and hardships. The most famous of these is the bridge at Luding (see p324) where Mao's army was pinned down by heavy machine gun fire, but managed to survive thanks to the heroic actions of a band of martyrs.

In 1935, the Communists crossed from Sichuan into Shaanxi. Against all the odds, the Communists had lived to fight another day. In 1935, Mao wrote:

The Long March is a manifesto. It has proclaimed to the world that the Red Army is an army of heroes, while the imperialists and their running dogs, Chiang Kai-shek and his like, are impotent. It has proclaimed their utter failure to encircle, pursue, obstruct and intercept us. The Long March is also a propaganda force. It has announced to some 200 million people in eleven provinces that the road of the Red Army is their only road to liberation.

One of the leading Communists on the march was a quiet, unassuming man from West Sichuan by the name of Deng Xiaoping (see p89). Although at this point he was a fairly minor player in the CPC's leadership, he would soon rise to achieve a position of prominence unrivalled by any Sichuanese person since.

The War of Resistance Against Japanese Imperialism

The Japanese initially invaded northeast China in September, 1931, but it wasn't until several years later that they solidified their hold on the region and reinstated the puppet Emperor, Puyi. On July 3, 1937, Japan began to expand, attacking the Chinese at Lugou Bridge. This marked the beginning of the War of Resistance.

Chiang Kai-shek and his Nationalists were forced, due to lack of support and accusations that they were too busy hunting down Communists, to sign a peace treaty with the CPC. By this point, the Guomindang had been pushed as far back as Chongqing, and the city was bombarded. Chengdu also suffered under the advance of the Japanese, being bombed and bombarded numerous times.

However, the flight of the Guomindang to Sichuan proved a boon for the province. They brought with them numerous academics, thinkers, and businesspeople who stayed on after the war to help rebuild. This influx of money and talent helped Chengdu to grow, prompting its resurgence as a major financial and industrial centre.

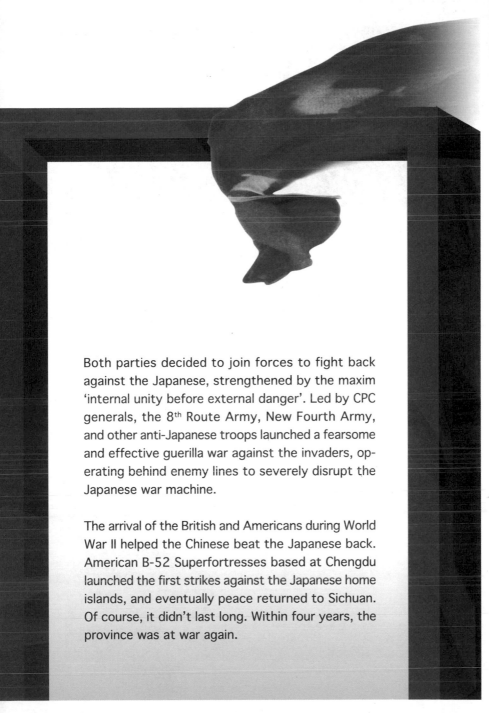

Both parties decided to join forces to fight back against the Japanese, strengthened by the maxim 'internal unity before external danger'. Led by CPC generals, the 8th Route Army, New Fourth Army, and other anti-Japanese troops launched a fearsome and effective guerilla war against the invaders, operating behind enemy lines to severely disrupt the Japanese war machine.

The arrival of the British and Americans during World War II helped the Chinese beat the Japanese back. American B-52 Superfortresses based at Chengdu launched the first strikes against the Japanese home islands, and eventually peace returned to Sichuan. Of course, it didn't last long. Within four years, the province was at war again.

The People's Liberation War, and the Foundation of New China

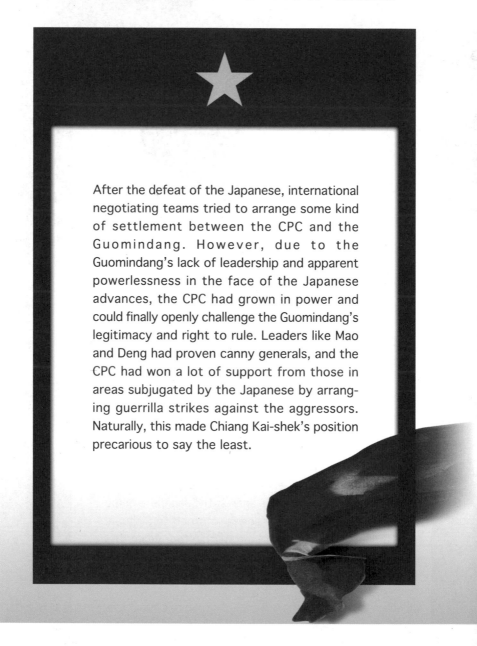

After the defeat of the Japanese, international negotiating teams tried to arrange some kind of settlement between the CPC and the Guomindang. However, due to the Guomindang's lack of leadership and apparent powerlessness in the face of the Japanese advances, the CPC had grown in power and could finally openly challenge the Guomindang's legitimacy and right to rule. Leaders like Mao and Deng had proven canny generals, and the CPC had won a lot of support from those in areas subjugated by the Japanese by arranging guerrilla strikes against the aggressors. Naturally, this made Chiang Kai-shek's position precarious to say the least.

In 1946, the Guomindang attacked the Communist bases in Yan'an and Manchuria, leading to a three-year period of civil war in which the Communist forces won victory after victory, slowly pushing the Nationalists out of China and into Taiwan and Hong Kong. The support of the masses in the liberated regions, help from student movements in areas under Guomindang control, and the active co-operation of several of China's most notable non-Party-affiliated public figures helped the CPC to oust the Guomindang,

During the three years of conflict, the Guomindang found their forces, numbering somewhere near the 8-million mark, utterly smashed by the much smaller PLA. After successful campaigns across China, the CPC finally crossed the Yangtze to begin rounding up the last of Chiang Kai-shek's forces.

The last bastion of Guomindang resistance on the Chinese mainland was based in Chengdu. Here, Chiang and his generals led a desperate defence against Mao's forces, but in the end the city fell to the Communists. The Guomindang leaders fled to Taiwan, and in October Mao proclaimed the birth of the People's Republic of China.

Modern Sichuan

With Mao in charge, life in China slowly began to improve. Between 1950 and 1953 China, with Sichuan included, underwent a transformation with regards to agricultural land. For the first time, farmers inherited the lands they had worked on all their lives. This act saw the first narrowing of the previously dramatic gap between the rich and poor that had characterised China's demographics until this point. China was finally becoming a fully-fledged Socialist state.

In the following years, the entire country began to industrialise and workers began vast rebuilding projects. The country's socialist mentality grew across the board, and in 1958, Mao launched the Great Leap Forward, a campaign to increase the agricultural and industrial output of the country. Mao's objective with regards to the Great Leap Forward was to maximize China's agricultural output by taking advantage of the country's huge manpower reserves, rather than relying on heavy machinery.

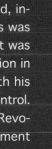
Zhou Enlai

In the years following the Great Leap Forward, industrial output continued to increase and this was followed in 1966 by the Cultural Revolution. It was Mao's intention to renew the spirit of revolution in China, and bring the country more in line with his Communist policies, but it quickly ran out of control. Nowadays many in the West see the Cultural Revolution as a disaster, but the Chinese government studied the results and, once order was restored, learned from their mistakes. In many ways, in the aftermath of the Cultural Revolution China began to gear itself for the heavy development it would experience from here on in.

From 1973 political unrest between the Maoists and the moderates led by Premier Zhou Enlai and Deng Xiaoping continued, until Deng finally emerged as China's Premier after Mao's death in 1976. Deng's economic policies saw China opened to the rest of the World, an act that attracted considerable foreign investment and caused a rapid advancement in the world of modern technology. China, and Sichuan in particular, entered an era of building and prosperity and the agriculture industry boomed.

In 1997, the Government split Chongqing and Sichuan, with Chongqing becoming its own municipality. The move was considered vital to the growth and development of China's southwest region.

Deng Xiaoping

The Lie of the Land

Sichuan is one of China's largest and geographically most isolated provinces, and its 485,000 square kilometres of land are as diverse as its eclectic mix of inhabitants. Located in south western China, this landlocked province is bordered on all sides by natural frontiers, which have acted as barriers over its long history, helping to create and retain the unique character of the 87.5 million people who call it home. To the east the vast Sichuan Basin, which houses the capital city of Chengdu, is surrounded by lofty mountains, while to the west, the highland peaks stretch away into Tibet. At an altitude of over 4000m above sea level, this upland plateau forms an inhospitable boundary, which combined with the main body of the Qinghai and Tibet plateaus to the north is one of China's most inaccessible and impressive ranges. To the south of the province, the northern section of the Hengduan Range completes the mountainous barricade that has come to geographically define Sichuan. The Gongga Mountain is Sichuan's highest peak, rising to a staggering 7556m above sea level. Located approximately 320km from Chengdu it is also home to Asia's lowest glacier.

More than 1300 rivers soar through the valleys and Sichuan Basin, most belonging to the Yangtze River system. The Jinsha River weaves its way across the southern stretches of the province from southwest to northeast until reaching the city of Yibin. At this point it becomes known as the

World famous super-river, the Yangtze. The notably large Jialing, Min, Tuo and Wujiang rivers feed into the Yangtze from both north and south. Together, this network of powerful rivers forms a natural water transport system within Sichuan, with Leshan, Yibin and Luzhou being the major cities along the trunk waterways.

Sichuan's vibrant capital Chengdu is located in the centre of the province, nestled in the western fringes of the Sichuan Basin. It is often referred to as the 'Land of Milk and Honey' due to its prime location amidst the fertile agricultural lands that have seen Sichuanese people largely escape past famines that have ravaged large portions of the country. The verdant basin has often seen Sichuan characterised as a predominantly rice-growing region, and this is certainly true of much of the lowlands. It is, however, a major producer of crops such as corn, sweet potatoes, wheat, rapeseed, barley, soybeans and millet. Tropical fruits such as the lychee and citrus fruits flourish as do apples and pears grown in the cooler temperate climates. In the western areas grazing land is in abundance, and cattle and pig populations are the largest in the country. Other livestock raised in Sichuan include yaks, horses, sheep, and goats. Throughout history Sichuan has been referred to as the 'Province of Abundance' with grain, rice and pork outputs topping those of all of China's provinces.

Despite its harsh highland terrains, Sichuan boasts 89,000km of highways, 1,152km of which are fast, efficient expressways. The vast majority of expressways lead to and from Chengdu and have sped up traffic into and out of this busy, prosperous city with many top tourist destinations now but a few hours away. Chengdu is also home to the Chengdu Shuangliu International Airport, one of China's busiest airports. In addition, Sichuan has six domestic airports including the recently constructed Jiuzhaigou airport, which has drastically opened up the northern reaches of the province to tourism. Five trunk railway lines operate within the province including the Chengdu – Chongqing, Chengdu – Kunming and Baoji – Chengdu lines. Several intra-province lines combine to form a total of 2,693km of railway.

Sichuan has a strong economy with a GDP of US$103 billion and is one of the major industrial bases of China. Its main industries include electronics information, hydropower, machinery, iron and copper smelting, coal mining, chemicals, medicine and food processing. Sichuan is also a major cotton producer. In recent years tourism has dramatically increased and Sichuan is fast becoming one of the country's most popular destinations, both with Chinese and foreign tourists. Sichuan is also known for its cottage industries including hand woven cloth, silk products, embroidery and silver and copper smithing.

Sichuan abounds in natural resources boasting 123 different minerals. It leads the country in reserves of vanadium, titanium, calcium, mirabilite, fluorite, natural gas and sulphur iron. It is the world's leading producer of titanium and its hydropower reserves are second only to Tibet with a production of 150million kilowatts.

Sichuan provides some of China's most outstanding scenery, and key to its overwhelming popularity is its geographical diversity. Within the mountainous walls, Sichuan is a relative pictorial dictionary of geological formations. Plateaus, mountains, ravines, valleys, hills, plains, rivers, lakes, hot springs, waterfalls, glaciers and limestone caves barely scratch the proverbial surface of an endless list.

Climate

Sichuan's climate varies drastically from west to east. The eastern lowlands have a sub-tropical, humid, monsoonal climate with thick fog a frequent feature, while the western highlands see a more temperate-subtropical climate. While sunlight is intense, temperatures in the west of the province are considerably lower than eastern areas. The northern mountains serve to insulate the province from continental cold air in winter, providing a generally sub-tropical climate and over 300 frost-free days a year. The lowland region sees 1000mm of rain per year, with 500 – 700 mm falling on the highland plateau.

- - - - - - - - - - - - - - - - - -

Average temperatures

	Lowlands	Plateau
January	3 to 8°C	-9 to 3°C
July	25 to 29°C	1 to 17°C

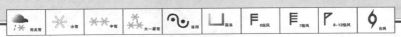

Nature and Conservation

Nature and Conservation

When asked what is Sichuan's most famous feature, Chinese people will, without hesitation and with a smile on their faces, say the Giant Panda. 80% of the world's pandas live in Sichuan and are considered highly endangered, with only 1596 left in the wild worldwide. The Sichuan and Chinese governments, along with international aid, are working tirelessly to see these much-loved creatures reintroduced in great numbers back into their natural habitats.

While the Giant Panda undoubtedly takes centre stage with regards to wildlife conservation, serious efforts are being made to protect countless other endangered species of animals and plants. Leopards, golden eagles, black ibis, golden monkeys and white-lipped deer are among some of the species that have found themselves under first class protection, with others such as the Tibetan macaque, black bear, otter and Asian golden cat under second class protection. In total, Sichuan is home to over 1000 species of vertebrates and 55 kinds of rare or endangered animals, including the world's biggest variety of pheasants. Sichuan occupies just 7% of China's land yet is home to 45% of its vertebrate species and 41% of its mammal species.

Forest covers 7.4 million ha of the province and a vast variety of vegetation thrives in the varied landscapes and climatic regions. The province is home to one fifth of the country's Down Redwood trees and Cathaya argyrophylla, two species so old they are considered living fossils. A ban on commercial logging was successfully introduced by the Sichuan government following devastating flooding in 1998 that ravaged areas along the Yangtze downstream from Sichuan. The ban has not only served to protect the river's upper watershed forests but has also eliminated what had been the major threat to pandas and other species of animals.

Amongst Sichuan's many accreditations is its number of highly protected cultural and natural heritage sites. The province proudly boasts five UNESCO protected sites, on a par only with Beijing. There are two World Cultural and Natural Heritage sites, 21 State-class scenic areas, 28 national forest parks, 40 nature reserves and 44 provincial-class scenic areas.

UNESCO protected sites

1 – Huanglong Scenic Area
2 – Jiuzhaigou National Park
3 – Mount Emei and Leshan Giant Buddha
4 – Mount Qincheng and Dujianyuan Irrigation System
5 – Sichuan Giant Panda Sanctuaries (of which there are seven nature reserves and nine scenic parks)

Panda Profile

The Giant Panda is today one of China's most famous faces. Having usurped the traditional dragon, pandas seem to be today's Chinese symbol, and are considered a 'national treasure'. Conservation efforts have awarded China great international praise, with numbers of this critically endangered creature slowly increasing, and have played an unwitting but crucial role in diplomatic relations. Sichuan is the proud home to the vast majority of the world's population of Giant Pandas and a trip to the province is incomplete without a visit to one of the reserves, where even the most apathetic of visitors will leave with a smile on their face. As one of the 2008 Olympic mascots, the panda's gentle character represents honesty, tolerance and gentleness, and they are seen as indications of peace and fortune.

Distribution and Habitat

The approximately 1600 wild pandas left in the wild are found predominantly in the mountainous regions of the Sichuan Tibetan plateau, as well as small populations in Gansu, Shaanxi and Tibet. They inhabit bamboo forests between 1200 and 3600m above sea level.

Diet

Historically pandas were carnivorous and still to this day retain a carnivore's digestive system. Today however pandas are herbivores eating bamboo and very little else. Due to their inability to process cellulose, they absorb very little energy and protein from bamboo and hence need to eat vast quantities to sustain themselves.

Reproduction

Pandas reach sexual maturity at 5 – 7 years of age and mating occurs in spring. A female gives birth to between one and three cubs in late summer or early autumn, although gestation periods vary widely. Mothers will generally only raise one cub even if she gives birth to multiple offspring. In captivity, pandas have twins 40% of the time. Cubs are tiny at birth, vastly disproportionate to the size of the female compared to most other mammals (1/900th the size) and will stay with their mothers for one and half to three years.

Behaviour

Pandas are mainly solitary with the exception of female and cub groups. Both males and females have home ranges and while a male's range can overlap with a female's, there is significant competition between males. It has however recently been discovered that outside of the mating season groups of males and females do meet to interact and socialise. In the wild pandas spend most of their day looking for and eating food and resting. Being from a temperate climate, they do not hibernate.

Status

The giant panda is listed on the World Conservation Union's (IUCN's) Red List of Threatened Animals as endangered. There are an estimated 1600 left in the wild (although numbers are growing thanks to fervent conservation efforts) and 221 in captivity in China.

Culture and Ethnic Minorities

Culture and Ethnic Minorities

Sichuan's large and unevenly distributed population is characterised by its diverse ethnicity. Of China's 55 recognised ethnic minorities, 53 of them are represented in Sichuan province. All of China's ethnic minorities are defined by a distinct language, a recognised indigenous homeland, a strong sense of identity and distinctive customs.

While the Han Chinese are of vast majority in both China as a whole and in the Sichuan province, there are a further 14 groups within Sichuan with populations exceeding 4,000.

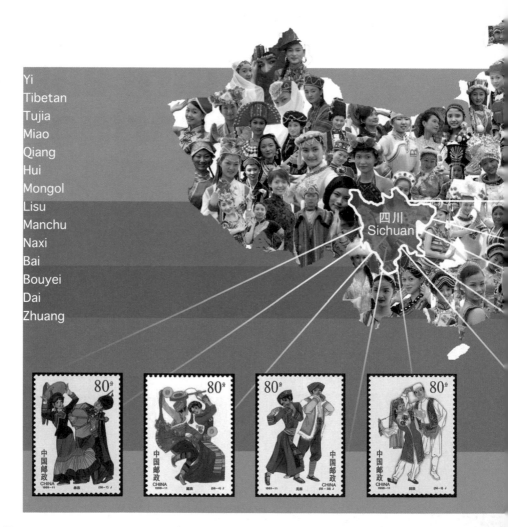

Yi
Tibetan
Tujia
Miao
Qiang
Hui
Mongol
Lisu
Manchu
Naxi
Bai
Bouyei
Dai
Zhuang

四川
Sichuan

Sichuan is home to China's second largest population of Tibetan people after Tibet itself, and is also the largest region inhabited by the Yi people. It is also the only region in the country where Qiang people live in homogenous groups.

While travelling throughout the province, the presence of this multitude of ethnic minorities and cultures is starkly obvious, as is the harmonious interaction between them. It is not uncommon within one town to find several different groups, often adhering to different religions, living peacefully amongst one another, managing to retain their own traditions, cultural practices and religious beliefs from one generation to the next.

Tibetan People

Population:

There are 5 million Tibetans living in China, half of which live in the Tibet Autonomous Region. Significant communities also exist in Qinghai, Gansu and Yunnan as well as Sichuan. Inside China they are known as Zang people.

Economy:

Agriculture and animal husbandry form the core of Tibetan people's economy and the mountains, grasslands and highland plateaus that are home to the largest communities are conducive to the rearing of vast yak, sheep, goat and pien cattle herds, and the growing of cold resistant barley is their main crop.

Language:

the widely spoken Tibetan language belongs to a sub-branch of the Tibetan-Burman language family. Three major geographical distributions have given way to three main dialects; Weizang, Kang and Ando. The Tibetan script was formed in the 6th century and contains four vowels and 30 consonants. Three differing styles of language are used to express levels of politeness, a remnant of the strict caste system of old.

Religion:

The Tibetans are Lamaist Buddhists. Buddhism began to establish itself in Tibet around 620AD after the arrival of missionaries from India. After hundreds of years of competition between Buddhism and the traditional Bön religion, Buddhism won out although many Bön aspects were incorporated. Religion plays a fundamental role in daily life and Tibetan people are devout believers in their faith. From the age of five, young boys enter monasteries by the thousands in order to study Buddhism and become monks.

Customs:

Male-centered, monogamous families are the norm and marriage is strictly intra-class (remnants of the ancient serf system). Sky burials, or *jhator,* are the most common form of burial and involves the cutting up of the body to be fed to birds of prey from atop mountains. Tibetan medicine plays an important role in society and doctors are well known for their veterinary treatments. In general, Tibetans go by their first name and not surname, and names are usually indicative of gender.

Dress:

Both men and women wear traditional dress, and decorative adornments and big, colourful items of jewellery are popular for both sexes. Men often wear coils atop their heads and both men and women often sport fur hats. Cloth or silk jackets are tied around the waist by a belt and all wear either wool or leather boots.

Festivals:

The most important Tibetan festival is the New Year when they dress in their finery and visit monasteries in order to receive blessings. Individual towns celebrate different festivals, the most popular Sichuan ones being the Tagong and Litang horse festivals.

Yi People

Population:

Over 1 million of China's 8 million Yi people live in the rural, mountainous regions of Sichuan in an area south of the Dadu River and along the Anning River.

Economy:

Most are farmers, herding cattle, sheep and goats, or work as nomadic hunters. Yi areas are generally rich in natural resources such as coal, iron, gold, silver, aluminium and several non-ferrous metals. Huge forests are home to many species of trees and plants with good economic value.

Language:

The Yi language is a Tibetan-Burman language which is closely related to Burmese. In the past, the Chinese government combined several groups speaking six different languages under the umbrella title of Yi and now communities differ widely from place to place. It is not uncommon for members of differing communities not to be able to understand each other.

Religion:

Yi people are generally animists, worshipping the spirits of their ancestors as well as those of nature. Exorcism, healing, praying for rain and the cursing of enemies are based on magic, and it is believed that dragons protect the villagers from evil spirits. Following a death, a pig or sheep is sacrificed on the house threshold to help maintain a strong bond with the deceased.

Miao People

Population:

Of a total 9.6 million Miao people, 130,000 reside in the Sichuan province, one of the largest ethnic minorities of south west China. They live in close communities in high or mountainous areas where the climate is mild and there is an abundance of natural resources.

Language:

The Miao speak a language belonging to the Miao-Yao branch of the Chinese-Tibetan language family. There are three main dialects spread over three regions; west Hunan, east Guizhou and Sichuan and Yunnan, a result of large-scale migrations over many centuries. Due to close contact with Han Chinese over many years, most also speak Chinese.

Customs:

The Miao family is small, patriarchal and monogamous. Marriages are usually arranged but young people do have the freedom to date. If a couple feels an attraction they exchange love tokens but must still win parental approval to marry. Occasional mass courting ceremonies are held during festivals where women from one village will gather to sing to men from neighbouring settlements. Miao people enjoy singing and dancing and have a rich tradition of folk literature. They are renowned for their colourful arts and crafts, notably embroidery, weaving, batik and paper cuts. Today many of these handicrafts are exported.

Dress:

Sichuanese Miao men wear short, button-down jackets, long trousers with a wide belt and long, black scarves. Women's dress varies, but in Sichuan women normally dress in high-collared short jackets and full or half-length pleated skirts.

Festivals:

Different communities celebrate different festivals or even the same festivals on different dates. Dragon Boat festivals and the Mountain Flower Festival (May 5th) are the most important, the latter being where childless parents go to pray to the god of fertility.

Lisu People

Population:

Of the 630,000 Lisu people, most live in concentrated communities in the counties of north western Yunnan, while others are more dispersed. Communities thrive in the Xichang and Yanbian communities of Sichuan, living alongside the Han Chinese, Bai, Yi and Naxi peoples.

Language:

The Lisu language belongs to the Chinese-Tibetan language family. In 1957, a new alphabetic script was created.

Economy:

As the Lisu generally inhabit mountainous areas alongside rivers, their main industry is farm crops while the forests near their settlements are rich in plant and animal species.

Religion:

In the past Lisu people worshipped many gods in a form of totemism, and religious professionals earned a great deal from performing sacrifices to ghosts

and fortune-telling. Christianity, spread by missionaries, was adopted in the mid-19th century and today 40% are Christians and 60% mostly atheists.

Customs:
Lisu people live in monogamous, patriarchal families and marriages are arranged by parents with huge betrothal gifts. Burial is the sole form of funeral practice. A man is buried with his cutting knives, bows and quivers while a woman has her weaving tools and cooking utensils hung over her grave.

Dress:
In most areas people wear home-spun hemp clothing. Women wear brightly-coloured head decoration and vibrant necklaces while men sport black turbans.

Festivals:
Festivals are similar to those of their closest neighbours, the Han, Bai and Naxi peoples. The Lunar New Year is celebrated by the feeding of cattle with salt to thank them for their labour. The Torch Festival and Mid-Autumn Festival (6th and 8th months of the Lunar calendar respectively) are also celebrated.

Qiang People

Population:

Sichuan is home to 300,000 Qiang people who mainly reside in the north west of the province in the mountainous counties of Maoxian, Wenchuan, Lixian, Beichuan and Heishui. Communities are generally comprised of 30 – 100 households forming 'fortress villages'.

Economy:

In the small valley plains where fortress villages cluster, people cultivate crops, hunt animals or collect mushrooms and herbs. Yaks and horses are herded on mountain-top pastures.

Language:

Qiang people speak one of two languages, both which derive from the Qiangic sub-family of Tibetan-Burman. As the two languages differ considerably, Chinese is often used to communicate between different groups.

Customs:

In Qiang marriages the woman is often older than her husband and this, combined with taking a leading role in agriculture, has led to a somewhat matriarchal society with women acting as head of the family and society. Romantic love and marriage are considered important and marriages are no longer arranged. The Qiang people abide by strict taboos with regards to birth and death. Before the birth of her baby a pregnant woman cannot go near the river or well nor attend a wedding or funeral. Following the birth, the mother may not enter the kitchen for one month nor leave the house or speak with strangers for 40 days. Strangers are not allowed in the house for one week following the birth and a flail or bamboo basket for boys and girls respectively is hung on the gatepost as a signal. Typically, a cow is sacrificed at the baby's naming ceremony.

Religion:

Most Qiang people follow Rujiao, a polytheist religion although those living nearer Tibet often follow Tibetan Buddhism. There are also small communities of Muslim and Taoist Qiangs.

Naxi People

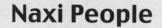

Population:

Most of the 300,000 plus Naxi people live in Lijiang Naxi Autonomous County in Yunnan, although there are significant populations in the Yanyuan, Yanbian and Muli counties of Sichuan. It is believed the Naxi originated from Tibet and are culturally a mix of Tibetan and Han Chinese influences as well as some indigenous features.

Language:

The Naxi language belongs to the Chinese-Tibetan language family. The Naxi pictographic characters known as 'Dongba' script and a syllabic writing known as 'Geba' script were created over 1000 years ago and used to record folklore, legends, poems and religious texts. However, in 1957 the Chinese government helped the Naxi people design an alphabetic script due to the difficulty of mastering the Dongba and Geba scripts.

Art and literature:

The Naxi people have a long and rich cultural, artistic and literary tradition. The famous 'Dongba Scripture' for example, dates back to the Tang Dynasty while the 'Baishaxiyue', an ancient musical composition, dates to the Yuan Dynasty. The Naxi enjoy singing and dancing, and weddings and funerals are a time of joy. Their most common musical instruments are flutes, reed pipes and wind string instruments.

Religion:

In the past, most Naxi people followed the Dongba religion which was a form of shamanism and Dongba sorcerers performed chants at weddings, funerals and festivals. Today, the Dongba religion still has considerable influence over society and Dongba lamas, or wise men, preach of harmony between man and nature. Through Han and Tibetan cultural influences, many Naxi adopted Tibetan Buddhism and, to a lesser extent, Taoism.

Customs:

Among the Naxi people of Yanyuan County in Sichuan there still exist faint remains of their past matriarchal society. Until the beginning of the democratic reform women were the heads of the family and society. Cremation was traditionally the sole form of funereal practice until the Qing Dynasty when some communities began to adopt burial.

Dress:

Women wear wide-sleeved loose dresses, jackets and long trousers underneath. They adorn themselves with highly decorated belts and sheepskin is worn slung over one shoulder. Men's clothing is more sedate and they usually dress much like that of the Han Chinese. Dongba lamas are easily recognisable in dress resembling that of the Bön priests of Tibet with distinctive conical hats decorated with a piece of red cloth.

Festivals:

The Sanduo Festival held on February 8th is celebrated in honour of the war God Sanduo who, according to tradition, defends the local people. It is believed he was born in the year of the goat so in respect of this, a goat is sacrificed in his honour. The Torch Festival is held on the 25th, 26th and 27th days of the 6th month of the Lunar Calendar (corresponding to early July on the Gregorian calendar).

Hui People

Population:

The majority of the Hui population is concentrated in northwest China but there are communities scattered across the country. Most Hui people are similar to the Han Chinese with the notable exception that they strictly follow the Islamic religion. Their origins are diverse and may be attributed to Mongol, Turkic or Persian merchants who settled in China in the 7th century.

Language:

Chinese is the native language although many have still retained certain Arabic or Persian words.

Customs and Religion:

Religious practices have influenced all aspects of Hui people's culture, customs and daily life. From living etiquettes to marriage and funeral customs Islam prevails. Perhaps the most notable differences to the Han Chinese are their dietary habits. Hui people do not eat pork, dog, horse and many birds and other foods considered delicacies by the Han Chinese. Funerals are simple affairs but many specific taboos are strictly observed. Wailing for example is not acceptable as it is seen as a complaint or as expressing hatred for the deceased. In general Hui people live a puritanical life where gambling, drinking and smoking are frowned upon and where even joking is not common practice. There is typically a mosque in every community and the Imam leads religious activities.

Dress:

In general Hui people dress the same as Han Chinese with notable headwear differences. Hui men wear traditional Muslim white caps while women wear headscarves covering their hair, some with veils.

Festivals:

There are three main festivals; Lesser Bairam (Kaizhai Festival) which is ends a month of fasting; Corban, which is celebrated on the 10th day of the last month of the Hui Calendar by the killing of an ox to give to the poor; and the Shengji Festival.

Religion

*S*ichuan's religious make-up is as complex, varied and fascinating as its diverse collection of ethnic minorities. Religious symbols are prevalent across the province and an eclectic mix of houses of worship form familiar landmarks in the landscape. What is instantly apparent upon travelling around Sichuan is the freedom these highly differing religious groups enjoy, being openly able to express their beliefs and practices, and the harmony and respect that each grants one another. In a world where religious conflict is a highly sensitive topic, Sichuan's harmonious co-existence, tolerance and mutual regard for one another's religious beliefs is refreshing, encouraging and perhaps beyond all, proof that peace is possible.

{ Tibetan Buddhism }

Tibetan Buddhism, or Lamaism as it is often referred to, is a form of Mahayana Buddhism that developed in Tibet and the surrounding Himalayan region in the 7th century. In 641, King Songsten Gampo united Tibet and took two Buddhist wives; Princess Wencheng of China and Princess Bhrikuti Devi of Nepal, an act that is considered the first, and possibly most significant, in China's Tibetan Buddhist history.

Beliefs: Tibetan Buddhism incorporates four main themes; the Madhyamika and Yogacara philosophy, tantric symbolic rituals, a Theraudian monastic discipline and the shamanistic elements of the indigenous Bön religion (see p79). The most dedicated of followers seek *Nirvana,* freedom from the cycle of reincarnation, but for the everyday follower the religion still retains certain shamanistic traits.

Practices: The religion includes a whole pantheon of Buddhas, bodhisattvas and Dharma protectors and meditation is an important feature. Unique hand gestures (*mudras*) and chanted *mantras* are often used to aid meditation, *Om Mani Padme Hum* being the most repeated. This most important of mantras can be found across all aspects of daily life in Tibetan Buddhist regions, in-scribed on stones and walls, counted on prayer wheels big and small and printed on banners and flags that are strewn across the landscape.

Symbols: The vast Tibetan Buddhist region of western Sichuan is quite liter-ally strewn with a colourful and vibrant array of Buddhist symbology. Decorat-ing every aspect of daily life, symbols form a vital role in Tibetan Buddhist religion and culture, and are one of the most noticeable and attractive fea-tures of these areas.

Eight Auspicious Symbols

 Endless Knot: representing the infinite wisdom of Buddha

 Lotus Flower: representing mental and spiritual purity

 Victory Banner: representing victory of the Buddha's teachings and wisdom over ignorance.

 Treasure Vase: representing spiritual and material abundance.

 Golden Fish Pair: representing good fortune, fertility and salvation

Parasol: representing royalty and spiritual power

 Conch Shell: representing the fame of Buddha's teachings.

 Wheel of Dharma: representing the teachings of Buddha.

Swastika: In addition to the Eight Auspicious Symbols, it is also common to see Swastikas painted on the sides of buildings, in temples and adorning statues and figures. It is also often used as decoration on clothing. As opposed to its formation in Nazism, Swastikas were (in the 20th century) changed to a left facing design. In Buddhism the swastika represents auspiciousness and good fortune as well as the Buddha's footprints and heart. The symbol on packaging often denotes suitability for vegetarians.

Taoism

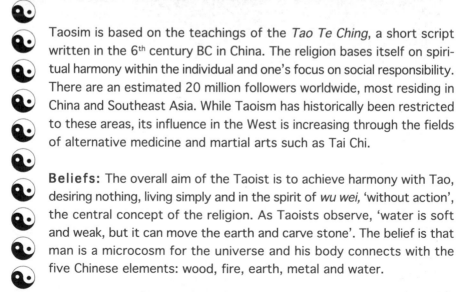

Taosim is based on the teachings of the *Tao Te Ching*, a short script written in the 6th century BC in China. The religion bases itself on spiritual harmony within the individual and one's focus on social responsibility. There are an estimated 20 million followers worldwide, most residing in China and Southeast Asia. While Taoism has historically been restricted to these areas, its influence in the West is increasing through the fields of alternative medicine and martial arts such as Tai Chi.

Beliefs: The overall aim of the Taoist is to achieve harmony with Tao, desiring nothing, living simply and in the spirit of *wu wei,* 'without action', the central concept of the religion. As Taoists observe, 'water is soft and weak, but it can move the earth and carve stone'. The belief is that man is a microcosm for the universe and his body connects with the five Chinese elements: wood, fire, earth, metal and water.

Practices: *Baibai*, a form of prayer involving bowing towards an altar whilst holding an incense stick in one hand, is widely practiced by Taoists. At certain times of the year, food is offered to gods and/or departed relatives as a sacrifice, while at other times lively street parades are held involving fireworks, floral floats and traditional music. Fortune-telling and astrology have also long been associated with Taoism.

Deities: Traditional Taoism is polytheistic and its deities are part of a hierarchy (and can be raised or lowered in importance). There are many disagreements about which deity is considered 'top', but contenders include the Jade Emperor, Laozi and the Three Pure Ones and Hong-jun lao-zu, the 'great primal originator'.

Symbols:
Yin-Yang (*Taijitu*): This is the most widely used and certainly the most easily recognised Taoist symbol and it is common to see it on flags, temple floors or stitched into clerical clothing.

Eight Trigrams *(Bagua):* These represent the main Taoist philo-sophical concept.

Tao: The Chinese symbol for Tao.
Another common symbol is that of a zigzag with seven stars. Taoists regard the poles as divine and this symbol represents the Big Dipper constellation.

Taoist temples fly square or rectangular flags and usually contain writing or diagrams. They act both as decorative items and talismans and traditionally a tree branch is used as a flagpole.

Confucianism

Confucianism is a way of life taught by Confucius in the 6th to 5th centuries BC. Due to its lack of specific rituals or religious practices, it is seen by some as a philosophy more than a religion, but this is highly debatable. Confucianism has been followed for more than two millennia in China, often alongside Taoism, Buddhism or other religions. It is estimated there are five to six million followers although this number is difficult to calculate given the tendency of Confucians to belong to more than one religious group, their life philosophy complementing other religious beliefs.

Beliefs and Principles: The main principle is *ren* 'humaneness' and is characterised by a very positive view of human nature. The elements of *li* (rituals), *zhong* (loyalty to a person's true character), *shu* (forgiveness) and *xiao* (faith) combine to form *de* (virtue).

{ Islam }

Ten different Muslim groups form the 200 million Chinese Muslims, the Hui ethnic group forming 48% of this figure. One of the most notable features of Muslim communities in China is the presence of female imams.

Beliefs: Islam is a monotheistic religion based on the revelations of the Prophet Muhammad in the 7th century. These were later recorded in the principle Islamic text, the Qur'an. Islamic practices centre around the Five Pillars of Islam; faith, prayer, fasting, pilgrimage and alms.

Mosques: Mosques differ considerably from one part of the country to the other. In Sichuan, mosque architecture often reflects that of local styles and mosques tend to have a more 'Chinese' appearance than those in other areas of the country, which more closely resemble Middle Eastern styles. There are four notable mosques in Sichuan; Chengdu Mosque, Langzhang Baba Mosque, Songpan Mosque and Xichang Mosque.

Christianity

Christianity in China has been developing since at least the 7th century and there are an estimated 16 million Chinese Christians, both Protestants and Catholics. Within Sichuan Province, Christianity is not as prevalent as in other regions and certainly takes a back seat to other, more highly represented faiths, notably Tibetan Buddhism and Taoism.

Bön

Bön was Tibet's indigenous religion long before the arrival of Buddhsim in the 7th century AD. Due to their distinct similarities, it is today a matter of great debate as to which influenced which. There are an estimated 100,000 followers, known as **Bönpo,** who practice today what is referred to as modern Bön, a form of Yungdrung Bön. There are an estimated 100,000 people (10% of Tibetans) who consider themselves members of the Bön order.

Original Bön: This term refers to the indigenous, shamanisitc religion of Tibet which was based on a belief that nature is pervaded by good and evil spirits.

Yungdrung (eternal) Bön: This is the second phase of the religion believed to have been founded by Shenrab Miwoche, a kind of Buddha. Tradition states he existed 18,000 years ago and lived in the mythical world of Zhang Zhung near Tibet. In the same way that Buddha renounced his royal life for the monastic life, so too did Shenrab Miwoche. He worked to achieve enlightenment and to teach others how to achieve it. The change in the Bön religion from one of animistic belief to Yungdrung is therefore attributed to this figure.

Modern Bön: There are considerable differences between Original and Yungdrung Bön and its modern, practiced form, and it now closely resembles Buddhist practices. Despite the changes from its Original and Yungdrung forms, followers still consider themselves part of the Bön tradition.

Practices: Bön practices are similar in many ways to Tibetan Buddhist practices, where the use of thangkas, mandalas and meditation to several deities is performed as a means to enlightenment. Monastic life forms a strong part of the culture and religion. Remnants of Original Bön can often been seen, with astrology and medicine remaining important features.

Dongba

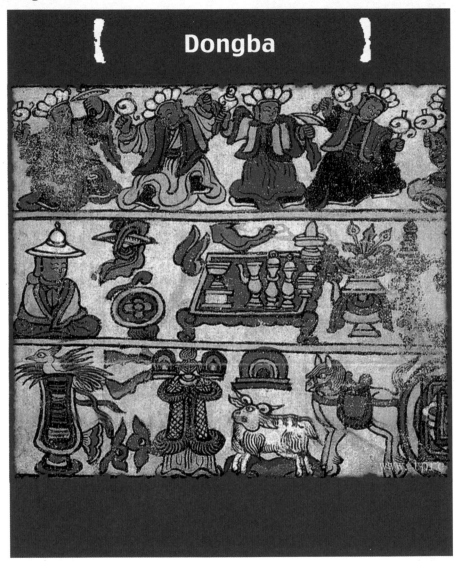

The Dongba religion is today practiced by the Naxi people of southwest China, many of whom live in Sichuan province (see p64). Believers or 'Dongba' (meaning 'the intelligent') are in effect a combination of shaman, scholar, artisan and craftsman and an important successor of the traditional Dongba culture.

Bön priests: The religious priests, who are referred to as Dongba, still exert considerable influence over the Naxi people, and are believed to be priests of the Bön religion. They teach of creating harmony between man and nature and their costumes bear striking resemblances to those of Bön and Tibetan Buddhist priests and monks. Pictures of Bön gods can often be seen adorning head wear, while Tibetan prayer flags and Taoist offerings are often used in rituals. Dongba are in effect combinations of witch doctor, scholar, artisan and craftsman, and the Naxi people see them as important successors to their traditional culture.

Beliefs: The Dongba religion is based on the belief that man and nature are in fact half-brothers, born to two different mothers but the same father.

Scriptures: Dongba has a highly developed and ancient script and the Dongba Scriptures consists of a vast amount of volumes. There are over 1,500 recorded types and over 20,000 volumes, which are displayed and collected in libraries and museums across China and the world. A large collection can be seen in the museum of Lijiang in Sichuan's neighbouring Yunnan province. The scriptures contain texts pertaining to philosophy, history, religion and medicine as well as astronomy, folklore, literature and art, and are considered a real encyclopedia of Naxi society and culture.

Sichuan's Hall of Fame

Zhuge Liang, the Hero of Shu

The *Three Kingdoms Romance* is one of China's greatest and most well-loved books. With a cast of characters plucked straight from history, the epic tells the story of one of China's most turbulent periods, and makes heroes and legends out of mortal men.

Yet among all the heroes immortalised in Luo Guanzhong's masterpiece, one stands supreme. A paragon of wit, wisdom and intelligence, Zhuge Liang's exploits have made him one of the most revered characters in China's literary and military history.

Zhuge Liang

The Real Zhuge Liang

Born into a poor family in Shandong Province in 181 AD, Zhuge Liang had it rough during the early years of his life. His parents had both died by the time he was twelve, and the warlord Cao Cao's aggressive expansion campaigns forced his family to flee to Longzhong. Zhuge made friends with many of the town's intellectuals, and he soon showed an aptitude for military thinking and wise counsel.

He married the daughter of a renowned local scholar and his reputation continued to grow culminating in Liu Bei, the legendary ruler of the Kingdom of Shu asking him to join his forces.

After Liu Bei pleaded with him three times, Zhuge Liang agreed to join him. He proved a canny military commander, fighting at the battle of the Red Cliffs, a vital turning point in the War of the Three Kingdoms. He advised Liu Bei on several victorious campaigns, but at the battle of Yiling, Liu Bei ignored his advice and suffered a disastrous defeat which led directly to his death.

Zhuge Liang was named Chancellor of Shu under Liu Bei's son, Liu Shan, and remained steadfastly loyal to his new lord. He reorganised the alliance with the kingdom of Wu that was vital to the two kingdoms' mutual survival, and came up with several brilliant inventions including an early wheelbarrow, and a form of semi-automatic crossbow.

After a successful campaign pacifying rebels in the south of Shu, Zhuge Liang turned his attention north, and led a series of expeditions against the kingdom of Wei. Despite Zhuge Liang's military skill, only one of these expeditions proved successful, the others suffering from freak bad weather and supply difficulties. On the fifth expedition, he died of overwork and illness in an army camp at the Battle of Wuzhang Plains at the age of 54.

Zhuge Liang: The Legend

In the *Three Kingdoms Romance,* Luo Guanzhong highly exaggerated Zhuge Liang's physical capabilities. He gave him magic powers, including the ability to command the weather, and several of the accounts of his exploits in the novel are completely fictional. Today, Zhuge Liang is more than just a general. He is a paragon of intelligence, courage, and virtue; a folk hero equal to El Cid, Charlemagne, or William Wallace. He continually pops up as a character in TV shows and role-playing games, and he is worshipped as a near-deity at Wuhou Temple (see p337)

Du Fu: Poet, Historian and Sage

Possibly the greatest of China's literary giants, Du Fu (712-770) lived a life that is in itself worthy of a novel. Displaced from his home a number of times by war and exile, he kept writing with a creative spirit and zeal that perfectly captures the atmosphere of life in the Tang Dynasty.

Du Fu was born in a village near the town of Luoyang, Henan Province, to a noble family that claimed direct descent from the Emperor Yao. However, the family was often very poor, and his mother died when he was very young. Du Fu was raised by an aunt and had a very close relationship with his four brothers and one sister who often appear in his poems.

Despite being educated to a reasonably high standard, he failed his first attempt at the civil service exams. He spent several years travelling, before returning to the capital of Chang'an and petitioning the emperor for the right to serve in court.

In 752 Du Fu married and had five children, though one later died in infancy. From 754 however, life started to go downhill for Du Fu. He was unemployed, developed chronic asthma, and was forced to move due to a series of massive floods in the region.

Du Fu

Arrival in Chengdu

In 755, Du Fu was finally granted a position at the Emperor's Court. However, before he could begin his duties, the An Lushan rebellion began and the Empire was thrown into turmoil. After several years on the move, he finally settled in Chengdu in 760.

It was here that Du Fu's career as a poet really began to take off, though he spent much of his time living in considerable poverty. He lived in a small thatched hut (see p141) and borrowed money on a regular basis from his friend Yan Wu, the governor of the city.

His greatest poems were written in Chengdu, and many of them are vivid accounts of the world he saw around him – the struggles, joys, and despairs of his neighbours and family.

Du Fu died in 770 in Tanzhou (now Changsha), before achieving the fame he truly deserved. Du Fu's poems are seen as both masterpieces of the poet's art, and a valuable insight into a turbulent period of Chinese history. Du Fu mastered all the forms of Chinese poetry, and often adapted the style of his prose to suit his surroundings.

Many liken the influence Du Fu has on Chinese culture and language to that of Shakespeare on English. His poems are taught in schools and his loyalty and desire to serve the state are cited as examples throughout the Chinese education system. By turns funny, dramatic, sad, angry and reverent, Du Fu's poetry is a symbol of Chinese culture, as valuable a national treasure as the Great Wall, the panda, and Tiananmen Square.

Deng Xiaoping, Sichuan's Favourite Son

Deng Xiaoping

Ask a class of Chinese university students who the most influential Chinese person of the 20th Century was, and you may be surprised at the answer. Although a few will pick sporting heroes like basketball player Yao Ming, or film stars like Jackie Chan, the likelihood is that two names will come up repeatedly.

Unsurprisingly, Chairman Mao will be one of them. The other will be Deng Xiaoping, alternately Mao's closest friend and greatest rival.

Deng Xiaoping was born on August 22, 1904 in Guang'an County, northeast Sichuan. His mother died when he was very young, and his father sent him to the famous Chongqing Preparatory School. He graduated at 15, and was selected to take part in an exclusive study-placement program in France.

An Introduction to Communism

Deng Xiaoping and Zhou Enlai

It was here, amidst stints as a fireman, car factory worker and student, that the young Deng met Zhou Enlai. Zhou was 6 years Deng's senior, and introduced him to the ideals of Marxism-Leninism. Deng joined the Chinese Communist League in Europe in 1921, and officially joined the Chinese Communist Party in 1923.

In October 1926, Deng returned to China. He was already actively involved in Chinese politics prior to his return, and when he came back he soon found himself at the forefront of the Chinese Communist Party. In 1928 he led the Baise Uprising in Guangxi province, directly challenging the Guomindang government. After the uprising was quelled, Deng joined the leaders of the party at Jiangxi.

The Long March

When the Guomindang surrounded the Communists in 1934, Deng was one of the 90,000 who set out on the Long March (see p26). During the march, Deng served as General Secretary of the Central Committee of the Communist Party, joining the upper ranks of the power structure that centered upon Mao.

During the war with Japan, and the subsequent Civil War with the Guomindang, Deng proved himself to be a canny general and strategist, as well as a shrewd politician. He spent a short time in Yan'an in 1938 before leaving to lead the sieges of Chongqing and Chengdu. During the sieges, the Guomindang's last bastions of resistance on the Chinese mainland were smashed, and the Guomindang and their leader, Chiang Kai-shek, fled to Taiwan.

When the People's Republic of China was officially founded in 1949, Deng was made First Secretary and asked to oversee operations in the southwest of the country. He negotiated several deals with Tibetan leaders, enabling China's emancipation of Tibet. For this he was named Secretary General of The Party, as well as being rewarded with several other important posts.

The Fall from Grace

Deng soon fell out of favour and was placed under house arrest in the countryside, but thanks to the influence of Zhou Enlai, by now China's Premier, he was brought back into the fold in 1974. This was short lived however as unrest soon reared its head between Deng and Mao supporters following Zhou's death.

After Mao's death in 1976, Deng began to emerge as a political powerhouse once again and launched a series of agricultural and industrial policies.

Deng Xiaoping   Mao Zedong

Deng's New China

It was Deng who announced that Mao's philosophy when in charge was '70 percent right, 30 per cent wrong'. During the 1980s, Deng reopened international trade and allowed foreign companies to open offices in China. He gained considerable renown on the internatioal stage when he met President Carter in 1979, and established himself as a charismatic and shrewd statesman.

Deng's domestic reforms were just as massive, instituting new policies across the board. The goals of Deng's reforms were summed up by the Four Modernizations: agriculture, industry, science and technology and the military. He also set up special economic zones to promote the growth and strengthening of the booming Chinese economy.

Officially, Deng decided to retire from the top positions when he stepped down as Chairman of the Central Military Commission in 1989, and retired from the political scene in 1992.

Deng Xiaoping died on February 19th, 1997 at age 92. There can be no doubt that Deng's legacy is still apparent in China, as the economic and social reforms he instigated continue to keep the economy booming. He is loved and revered by the Chinese, who see him as a symbol of stability and progress. He was twice named TIME Magazine's Man of the Year, and in 2000 was named Asia Week's Asian of the Century for Politics and Government, losing the title of Overall Asian of the Century by a small margin to Gandhi.

PRACTICALITIES

Out and About

When to Go

Sichuan has two very different climatic regions. Chengdu and the east have a subtropical climate and humid, rainy summer, while the highland plateau in the west sees a colder, drier climate. While it is possible to travel to the vast majority of the province at any time of year, severe weather conditions in the high uplands mean travel in the heart of winter may be limited. With temperatures reaching -9°C, many roads may be closed due to unsafe conditions, in particular parts of the Sichuan-Tibet Highways. Rain in the summer months in lower-lying areas can be disruptive to sight-seeing, and Chengdu's heavy, humid fog can be rather unappealing. The best time to visit the province as a whole is during the spring and autumn periods. September to November and March to May provide the most comfortable travelling. That said the upland regions are always considerably colder than Chengdu so warm clothes are a must at any time of the year.

On the Road

*D*espite its rough terrain and severe geology, Sichuan's transport network is generally very good. Chengdu is a modern and active city and transport in and around it is fast, easy and efficient. Expressways have made many of the major sights around the city an easy daytrip away and trains link the capital with neighbouring provinces. Buses are however the most popular form of intra-province transport. While buses leaving Chengdu offer comfort and great service, quality does tend to diminish the further you get from the capital. Highland areas offer reliable if decidedly agonizing services and vehicles tend to be old and tatty. They do however get you from A to B and are undoubtedly an experience not to be missed. Roads are under constant construction to make them more friendly on the skeletal system, but with such vast expanses to cover, most are barely more than a pot-holed, rocky track.

Out and About

The new Jiuhuang Airport now serves the northern tourist destinations of Jiuzhaigou, Huanglong, Songpan and surrounding areas and has shortened the previously 12 hour journey to 45mins.

Within towns and cities, taxis and pedicabs are the main forms of transport, and vary in quality and price (again dependent on their distance from Chengdu). While taxi drivers are generally honest and trustworthy, beware of scams from privately hired minivan drivers, especially out in rural areas. While the majority are fair, a common ruse is to agree on a price and then demand more money whilst en route because of bad road conditions, weather and whole host of other excuses. Sticking to reputable, licensed drivers and public transport is strongly recommended.

Accommodation

Sichuan is well geared towards tourism and the more popular destinations are teeming with hotels to suit any pocket. Establishments range from guesthouses and hostels to four and five star hotel complexes, and from the luxurious to the dreadful. In more remote, out-of-the-way locations (especially the far west), quality does wane somewhat, so don't expect the Ritz (or anything close!). Chengdu has some fantastic hotels and hostels, all at very reasonable prices, and makes a great base for exploring the surrounding areas. If you are visiting Sichuan during a national holiday or local festival such as the immensely popular Litang Horse Festival then be sure to book ahead. Prices during these times are highly inflated and rooms a scarce commodity. At any other time of the year you shouldn't have a problem finding somewhere to stay at late notice.

PRACTICALITIES

In the Know

Orientation

*E*nglish maps are hard, if not impossible, to come across outside of the capital, and in any case most locals cannot point you in the right direction using one. Directions tend to be based on landmarks and not on streets, most being unnamed anyway. Having the name of your destination in Chinese characters is the only way to get any help from passers-by and is a must if you're trying to get a taxi.

Health

$\mathcal{A}$s with many parts of China, Western medicine hasn't yet made even a blip on the medicinal horizon and finding English-speaking doctors or Western medicine is almost impossible. The **Global Doctor Clinic** *Tel: 028-85226058* in Chengdu largely serves the ex-pat community and has 24-hour English speaking doctors. Outside of Chengdu however, traditional medicine, both Chinese and Tibetan, is all you will find. Be sure to take a first aid kit and any prescription medicine with you. Painkillers are a good idea to combat altitude-induced headaches in high regions.

Tap water is not drinkable anywhere in China and bottled water is widely available and extremely cheap. Food tends to be well-cooked, even in the most rudimentary of eateries, but if you have a sensitive constitution it is probably best to avoid meat dishes until you have got accustomed to the food (especially before a long bus journey where toilet stops are few and far between!).

The west of the province suffers from freezing temperatures for large parts of the year and intense sunlight. Cold, sunburn and altitude sickness in these areas are common so it is essential to be prepared and aware before you head off. Strong sunscreen, sunglasses and warm, wind resistant clothes are an absolute must, and altitude sickness medication is highly recommended.

Altitude Sickness

At heights above 2,440m altitude sickness can occur, and symptoms may be more likely or more severe the higher you go. It is important to give yourself plenty of time to acclimatise before attempting to do any strenuous activity or proceeding to a higher altitude.

Symptoms of altitude sickness can include headaches (mainly due to dehydration), lack of appetite, nausea or vomiting, fatigue, dizziness and/or insomnia. Analgesics can be taken to help with headaches and it is important to stay hydrated. If more serious symptoms such as fever, continued short-ness of breath, a dry cough, loss of consciousness or severe unrelenting head-aches occur it may indicate a more serious reaction to the altitude and it is important to seek medical help and get to lower ground. Most mountain climbers use the motto 'if symptoms increase, go down, down, down'.

Safety

China in general is a safe country for foreign visitors and violent attacks are extremely rare. Theft can occasionally be a problem so always keep hold of your belongings and don't leave valuables in hotel rooms, especially out in more rural areas. Tourists are often warned about trekking alone into remote areas and it is always best to take a guide. In general though, Sichuanese people are extremely inquisitive, and harmless staring is the most trouble you're likely to get.

Roads can be treacherous and driving techniques in rural areas leave a lot to be desired so if weather conditions are terrible, it's best to stay an extra day and wait for conditions to improve. Don't be worried about asking drivers to slow down if they are driving at break-neck speed, they don't get offended and will generally laugh and slow down. Remember though, these guys traverse the most awful of roads on a daily basis and are well aware of the dangers and, quite literally, pitfalls!

Money

*C*hengdu has no end of banks and money-changing facilities, ATMs are everywhere and credit cards are widely accepted. Bigger towns and more popular tourist destinations will have banks and ATMs but many rural areas don't. Kangding is the last stop for withdrawing money before heading out west, so be sure to bring cash along with you. Outside of the main towns most hotels do not accept credit cards, ATMs are obsolete and traveller's cheques cannot be cashed.

Internet

*I*nternet cafes are common even in the most remote and unlikely of places. Look for the sign 网吧 denoting internet. Connections tend to be fairly quick and reliable, but cafes can often be male-oriented, dirty and smoky. Many computers have headsets so international calls in remote areas can be made through free software programmes such as Skype.

Sichuanese Cuisine

Sichuanese Cuisine

Sichuan has been known since ancient times as the 'Land Of Abundance'. Thanks to the natural abundance of herbs, spices and seasonings, the fertile croplands of Dujiangyuan, and the large herds of farm animals, Sichuan has long been recognised as one of China's most vital agricultural resources.

Therefore it should come as no surprise that one of Sichuan's most famous exports is its unique local cooking style. Sichuanese restaurants show up in just about every city in China, and you'd be hard pressed to find a Chinese restaurant in the west that doesn't have at least one dish with the words 'Sichuan' and 'spicy' in it.

Of course, these paltry imitations don't even come close to the experience of eating Chengdu hotpot, or sitting down with the locals for a portion of yak's milk cheese dipped in sugar. The ever popular spicy Sichuan beef that is a staple on all Western-Chinese menus doesn't even feature in Sichuan restaurants!

In Sichuan the people have taken cooking beyond an art form or a necessity. It is an integral part of the culture, and without it Sichuan just wouldn't be the same.

The Spice of Life

The peppers that make Sichuan cuisine what it is today are actually a fairly new introduction to the gamut of spices used for cooking in the province. Arriving from Chile via India and from Portuguese traders in Macau during the 17th century, the *Fagara* (or Sichuan Peppercorn) thrived in the warm, humid climate of southwest China. Peppers had already been used here prior to this, but the fieriness of the Fagara kicked the level of spiciness up a notch.

According to old stories, the pepper became popular in Sichuan due to its ability to rid the body of 'inner dampness', caused by the humid air. The health benefits of the peppers are not understated: they are fantastic for the digestive system and contain vitamins C and A.

Menu Guide

Outside of Chengdu, ordering food can be a nightmare if you don't speak or read Chinese. Menus are very rarely translated into English and even picture menus, common in other parts of the country, are almost obsolete in Sichuan. Below are listed some of Sichuan's most popular and tastiest dishes to make ordering in a restaurant that bit more palatable.

Chengdu Hot Pot (Chengdu Huoguo 成都火锅)

Sichuan's most famous dish, Hot Pot is an eating style and an institution all to itself. A bowl of boiling water is placed in the middle of the table, swimming with all sorts of spicy goodness. Just pick what you want from the menu, and throw it in the pot, it's as simple as that!

Normally eaten by a group of people, hot pot is a fun, unique dining experience. Let your inhibitions go, dive in, and try a bit of everything.

One good tip is to make sure you have a Chinese person with you. A second is to only attempt this if you've mastered the basics of chopstick-handling... there are no knives and forks here!

Twice-Cooked Pork
(Huigourou 回锅肉)

This incredibly popular morsel is a favourite in northern Sichuan. Strips of fatty pork belly are stir-fried together with peppers, chives, chillies and garlic. While it may be big on cholesterol it is even bigger on flavour.

Kung Pao Chicken
(Gongbao Jiding 宫爆鸡丁)

The definitive Sichuanese dish, gong bao ji ding is a tangy jumble of chicken pieces, peanuts, leek and dried chillies, stir-fried and marinaded in a combination of sugar and vinegar. Swap chicken for shrimp and you have the equally delicious Kung Pao Shrimp (Gong Bao Xia Ren 宫爆虾仁).

Mapo Tofu (Ma Po Doufu 麻婆豆腐) *Suitable for Vegetarians*

With a name that translates roughly as 'Pockfaced Mother Tofu', you may be forgiven for being put off this Chengdu favourite. Soft pieces of tofu are marinated in a broth along with chilli powder, ground fagara, garlic, and ginger making it considerably tastier than its name implies.

Stir-Fried Beef & Ground Pepper (Qingjiao Niurousi 青椒牛肉丝)

Strips of tender beef and crisp peppers, stir-fried along with ginger, spring onion and soy sauce make this a perfect meal for one.

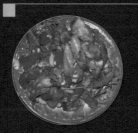

Spicy Fish & Onions (Cong La Yu Kuai 葱辣鱼块)

Fried chunks of fish fillet (usually carp), leek, and onion fried together in a spicy oil. The sheer simplicity of this dish makes it quite common, and often fairly cheap by fish standards.

Fish-Flavoured Aubergine (Yu Xiang Qiezi 鱼香茄子)
Suitable For Vegetarians

While not remotely fish flavoured, this blend of aubergine (eggplant), bean paste, vinegar and ginger makes for a nice break from the incredible spiciness of many other dishes.

Cold Saliva Chicken (Koushuiji 口水鸡)

A perfect appetiser, these strips of cold cooked chicken breast often come in a spicy, oily sauce. Usually this dish is covered in chopped scallion, pine nuts, and garlic.

Spicy Crab Soup (Xiang La Xie 香辣蟹)

A bowl full of spicy chilli broth, with a couple of whole hairy crabs thrown in for good measure. Don't be afraid to use your fingers to break the crabs open- just make sure you have a napkin handy!

And for the truly adventurous...

Mao Xue Wang (Mao Xue Wang 毛血旺)

So bizarre that it doesn't even have an English name, this dish is a steaming broth laden with unusual meats. It typically includes congealed pork blood, mutton and beef tripe, and beef oesophagus. The broth is also a monster - fagara, dried chilies, ginger and a spicy Sichuan sauce make this a real sweat-inducer!

And for those of you who just want something plain, a few all-around basic common Chinese dishes:

Boiled rice	*Mi fan* 米饭
Egg-fried rice	*Dan chao fan* 蛋炒饭
Aubergines (eggplant) and potatoes	*Tudou shao qiezi* 土豆烧茄子
Beef noodles	*Niurou mian* 牛肉面
Egg and tomato soup	*Xihongshi jidan* 西红柿鸡蛋
Steamed pork bun	*Xiaolongbao* 小笼包
Sauteed broccoli	*Suanrong xilanhua* 蒜蓉西兰花
Spinach and garlic	*Suanrong bocai* 蒜蓉菠菜

THE GUIDE

Chengdu

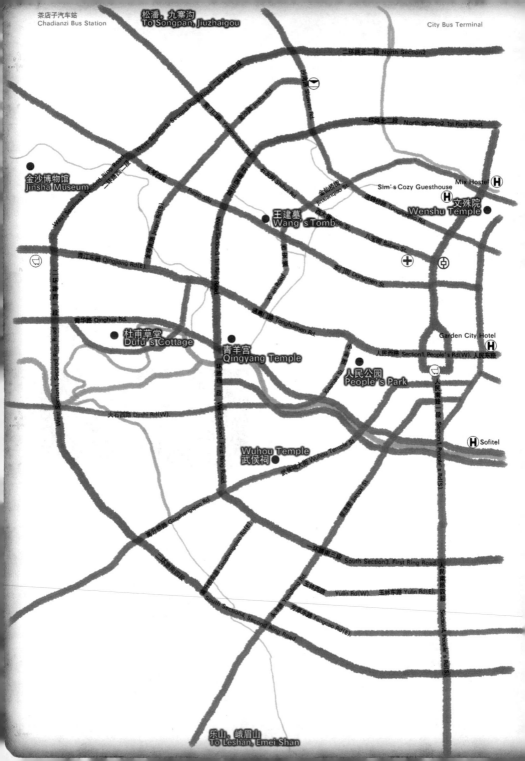

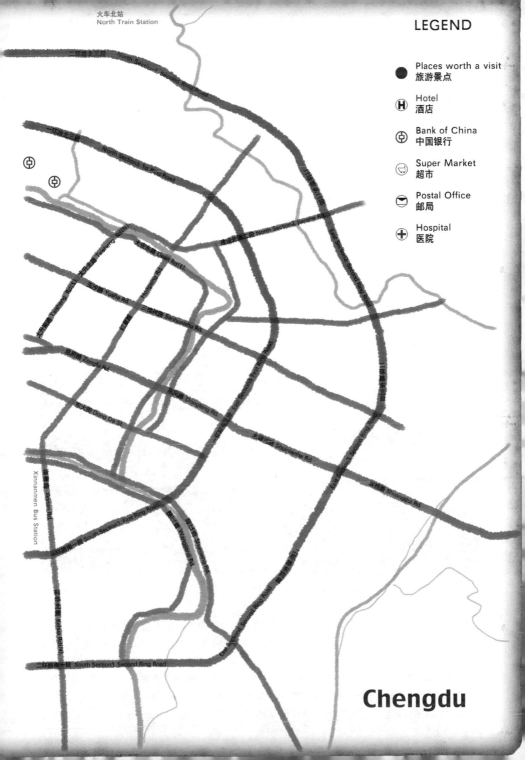

Chengdu 成都

*C*hengdu's 11 million strong population is one that has risen above the tests of time and always come out prosperous and content. Lying on the once volatile Sichuan Basin, great floods were long ago put under control with the construction of the Dujianyuan Irrigation System. From that date Chengdu hasn't looked back. Often dubbed the 'Land of Abundance' the city's people have escaped famines that have tormented other regions, the lands that encircle it forming the backbone of the country's rice production. Today the city is a vibrant, cosmopolitan hub where traditional values, world-famous spicy cuisine, cultural relics and a relaxed pace of life combine to form one of China's most popular cities. More recent titles such as 'China's Party City' have increased tourism and put it on the city weekend map. Bars and cafes outnumber those of Shanghai despite its comparatively smaller population, and Chengdu is embracing its new image, encouraging development alongside its traditional heritage.

Climate

Chengdu enjoys a warm, if not sunny climate. Protected to the north from the whipping Siberian winds by the Qingling mountain range, the climate is generally mild and humid. Hot, rainy summers see temperatures in the region of 30°C while mild winters see daytime temperatures of 10°C, much warmer than nearby cities. Chengdu does, unfortunately, suffer from an unappealing amount of cloudy days, and sunshine is a rarity.

Population

Chengdu is China's fifth-largest city in terms of population. With a total population of 11 million (4 million residing within the city proper), it falls in behind Chongqing, Shanghai, Beijing and Tianjin. While undoubtedly having emerged into the modern world along with its bigger counterparts, Chengdu has managed to retain its village atmosphere, where locals welcome visitors from home and abroad with open arms. The majority of residents are Han but an increasing number of people from other ethnic minorities as well as from Hong Kong and abroad have been settling in the city in recent years.

Economy

Sichuan, and Chengdu as its capital, has long been the mainland centre for traditional Chinese medicine. The majority of all Chinese medicines are produced and manufactured in Chengdu along with more recent investment in Western medicines. Hi-tech industries emerging from the province are seen as some of the best in the country and the city has become the financial centre for the west of China.

The Story So Far

*C*hengdu is an old city. It has existed in one way, shape, or form for the past 3,500 years. It has been the capital of four kingdoms, the site of the Guomingdang's last stand, and the home of some of China's greatest literary minds. *China Daily* recently voted Chengdu the fourth most liveable city in China, and the Chinese State Council lists it as one of the most important cities in China in terms of cultural and historical significance.

Early Chengdu

Chengdu started out as a simple settlement under the Ancient Shu civilisation. For a thousand years the city barely grew, remaining more or less the same size for generations. The people of Chengdu were simple farmers or herdsmen, and the city didn't even merit a wall for its own defence.

In the 4th century BC, King Kaiming, of Ancient Shu decreed that he would move his capital to the small town, aiming to emulate a legend in which a small village became the capital of a great kingdom. Sadly, it didn't go quite according to plan, and when the Qin subjugated the Shu, Chengdu was almost utterly destroyed.

Rebirth of a City

In its place, the Qin general Zhang Yi built a new city on the site of old Chengdu and surrounded it with a 25 metre high wall. This marked the beginning of modern Chengdu, and the city's growth was aided greatly some fifty years later when the legendary engineer Li Bing finished his vast irrigation project at Dujiangyuan. The growth in agriculture and improvements in water supply that arose from the project have allowed Chengdu to go over 2,000 years without drought or famine.

During the Han dynasty, the city was named Yizhou for a brief period. During this time, it became a regional trade hub, growing in size and

wealth. The city's brocade industry thrived at this time, and the city was affectionately known as "the brocade city" due to the unusual lustre of the brocade produced here. Many attributed this to the properties of the two rivers running through Chengdu, giving the brocade washed in them the gorgeous hues the town became famous for.

During the Three Kingdoms period, Emperor Liu Bei founded the kingdom of Shu in the province of Sichuan, and made Chengdu his capital. By now, the city had reverted to its original name, and was becoming a mighty walled settlement. Woodblock printing had become popular, and the city produced one of the oldest printed texts still in existence around 220AD.

The legendary minister and general Zhuge Liang held court in the city during the period in which he served as chancellor for Liu Bei and his son, Liu Shan. He orchestrated and planned his northern campaigns from Chengdu, and held a great love and respect for the city and its people.

War and Poetry

During the Tang dynasty, Chengdu emerged as a major centre for the arts, as well as warfare. The great poets Li Bo and Du Fu (see p141) both called the city home for a period during the tumultuous dynasty, and wrote many poems praising Chengdu's beauty.

One of Chengdu's most noted heroes from this period is Lady Huan Hua. The city's armies had been called to the Emperor's attendance in Changsha, so the lord of the city led his soldiers east, leaving the city defenceless. The Governor of Luzhou seized his chance to launch an assault against the city, sure of an easy victory. Lady Huan Hua, a Chengdu noblewoman, used her own family estate to raise an army and led them personally into battle against Luzhou. The attackers were repulsed, the city was saved, and Lady Huan Hua received an Imperial Knighthood.

Towards the end of the Song Dynasty, Chengdu was captured twice by different warlords, who set up their own kingdoms with the city as capital. Neither was particularly long-lived, and both times the city was quickly returned to Imperial control.

20th century Chengdu

The Second World War brought an unexpected wave of prosperity to Chengdu as the Nationalist government under Chiang Kai-shek fled to Sichuan Province to escape the invading Japanese forces. They brought with them businesspeople, workers and academics, who founded many of the industries and cultural institutions which continue to make Cheangdu an important modern business centre. During the latter stages of the war, American bombers were based in the city from which they launched bombing raids on the Japanese home islands. This offensive prompted the Japanese to withdraw from the Chinese mainland.

Chengdu was also the last city on the mainland to be held by Chiang Kai-shek and the Guomindang. In

July 1949, after a short siege, Chengdu fell to the Communist forces under Deng Xiaoping (see p91). This battle forced the Guomindang out of China and into exile in Taiwan, allowing the founding of the People's Republic of China.

Today Chengdu is a hub of business and trade, sporting a large international airport, a considerable ex-pat community, and an increasingly expanding commercial network. A thoroughly modern city, many of China's blue-chip and modern industries are based here. It is known around the world for the quality of its traditional Chinese medicinal practices, and is currently in the process of setting itself up as the economic hub of western China.

It will not be long before Chengdu achieves this goal, moving one step forward to being the 'Perfect City' the Kaiming envisioned three and a half millennia ago.

Accommodation

*C*hengdu has no lack of hotels and hostels to suit any taste, pocket or preference. It is generally a good idea to book ahead during Chinese holidays as the city's popularity is increasing by the year and rooms get booked up weeks ahead. As competition is intense, the city boasts a very high quality of accommodation for reasonable prices compared with other regions of the province where often a lack of choice means forking out for mediocre service and shabby rooms. Most of the major national and international hotel chains are represented in the city as well as a fabulous selection of top-notch, funky budget accommodation. Always ask about discounts, especially during quieter seasons.

Crash out

Mix Hostel *Address: 23 Renjiawan, Xinghuixilu, Wanfuqiao*万福桥星辉西路任家湾23号驴友记青年旅社*; Tel: 028-83222271; www. mixhostel.com; email: mixhostel@hotmail.com; 15-25RMB/dorm, 50RMB/single, 70RMB/double.* While not much to look at from the outside, the inside is a completely different story. Three floors of wood paneled rooms centre around a communal courtyard and there is a great roof terrace decked out in colourful cushions. English-speaking staff can help arrange Tibet tours and permits, tours to the Panda Research Centre and a whole lot more. Laundry facilities, free internet, book exchange and Western-style snack foods are just the beginning of the list of facilities on offer. The affiliated 3* Mix Hotel across the road offers more private accommodation and a step up in comfort.

Sim's Cozy Guesthouse 观华青年旅社 *42 Xizhushi St 西珠市街 42 号; Tel: 028-66316000; www.gogosc.com; email: simscozygh@yahoo.co.jp; price 15-35RMB/dorm, 50RMB/single, 70RMB/double, 100-200RMB/single or double rooms with en-suite bathroom and a/c.* Perfectly located in the heart of the city, Sim's is just a stone's throw from the Wenshu Temple. Cosy aptly describes this clean and extremely pleasant guesthouse which offers private rooms as well as dorms set within quiet gardens. English-speaking staff can help make any travel plans including Tibet Tourism Bureau permits, Songpan horse treks and flight bookings – their website is extremely informative. Facilities include bike rental, laundry, internet, restaurant, luggage storage and postage service.

Mid-range

Garden City Hotel 花园城大酒店 *8 Daye Road 大业路 8 号; price 340-440RMB/double;*
Fabulous value for money, the Garden City offers absolutely everything one could need including full Chinese and Western breakfast buffets, two restaurants, café, internet, travel service, fitness and massage centre, hair salon and nightclub as well as full room facilities.

Splash out

Sofitel Wanda *15 Binjiang Middle Road 滨江中路 15 号; Tel: 028-66669999; www.sofitel.com; sofitelwanda@sofitelchengdu.com; 2000RMB/double.* This is the absolute best money can buy and is absolutely flawless. Classically elegant, it has absolutely all the facilities one could wish for and a whole lot more thrown in for good measure.

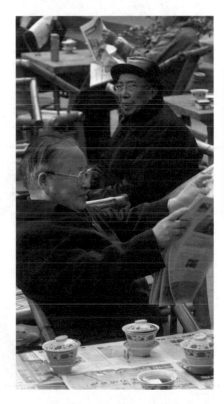

Stepping Out

*C*hengdu is a lively place of an evening; the city streets are lit up in a blaze of neon, seen-on-the-scene teenagers and partygoers stroll along the streets, and it seems everybody in the city goes out to eat at one of the zillion small restaurants tucked away at the side of the road.

Whether you want a bite to eat, something to drink or just to see some friendly faces, Chengdu has it all.

Fat Mother's Chongqing Hot Pot 胖妈火锅 *14 Dongsi St, Yihuan Rd* 成都成华区一环路东四段 14 号机建大厦 1 楼(姣子音乐厅旁); *around 100RMB for 6 people*

This amazing Sichuanese hot pot restaurant hasn't changed its name since before Chongqing seceded from Sichuan back in 1997, so don't be fooled. Offering a fantastic introduction to Sichuan's fabulous hotpot culture, Fat Mother's offers big tables, a sumptuous menu, and incredibly attentive staff, some of whom speak a little English.

The Sultan 苏坦土耳其餐吧 *1 Yulin Nanjie* 玉林南街 1 号; *Tel: 028-85554780; 80-100RMB for two people*

Tucked away off the main road in a small back street, the Sultan's large Turkish menu offers falafel, kebabs, and a wide range of other Arabic delights. The naan bread here is to die for and it is a rare, great vegetarian option as the menu incorporates plenty of meat-free dishes.

Jinli's San Gu Yuan Canteen 锦里·三顾园餐厅 *Jinli Lu, 231 Wuhoucidajie* 武侯祠大街 231 号锦里古街; *Tel: 028-66311388; dishes from 30RMB*

This upscale restaurant offers great traditional Sichuanese fare, in the mock-archaic surroundings of Jinli Lu. It is a great place to spend the evening people-watching (with the added benefit of a pictorial menu).

The Shamrock 三叶草爱尔兰西餐酒吧 *Renmin Nanlu, Section 4, Number 15* 人民南路 4 段 15 号; *Tel: 028-85226158; meals from 25RMB, Qingdao beer 25RMB/glass*

A friendly, bustling Irish bar, this watering hole is a second home to a large segment of Chengdu's expat community. Large TVs show live sporting events and the English-speaking staff are trained to a very high standard. The Western-style food is cheap, very good quality, and the portions are massive.

THE GUIDE

Dave's Oasis *21/1 Binjiang Zhonglu* 滨江中路 *21/1; Tel: 028-89500646; meals from 12RMB, Qingdao beer 15RMB/bottle.*

One of Chengdu's original drinking holes, Dave's is a laid-back backpacker hangout with comfy sofas, an awesome atmosphere and great food. Dave speaks great English and can give advice on all the things to see and do in Sichuan. Definitely a man to speak to, especially if you're planning some heavy backpacking.

The Leg & Whistle *Kehua Jie, Chuandahuayuan; Tel: 028-85461958; drinks from 20RMB*

This brand new British pub sports a fantastic selection of imported beers from all over Europe. Another comfortable hangout popular with the *waiguoren* (foreigners), the Leg has plans to offer food in the near future. When the taxi drops you off, look for a large flight of stone steps leading up onto the second level of a row of shops.

Chengdu Bookworm *Yujie East Road 2-7, Renmin South Road 28; Tel: 028-85520177 Qingdao 15RMB.*

The Bookworm, part of the successful Beijing-based chain, is just as comfy and cosy as its eastern cousin. Racks filled to bursting point with English language books line the walls, while the comfortable furniture and peaceful atmosphere make this the perfect place to enjoy a drink, a meal or just some quiet reading time.

On the Road

Air

Chengdu's Shuangliu International airport 成都国际机场 has daily flight connections with most Chinese cities and a growing number of international destinations. National and international destinations include Beijing (3 hours), Shanghai (2 hours), Chongqing (45 mins), Kunming (1 hour), Dalian (3 hours), Hong Kong (3 hours), Bangkok (3 hours) and Tokyo (6 hours). Several flights leave the domestic airport for Sichuan's Jiuhuang Airport, which serves the northern tourist destinations of Jiuzhaigou, Huanglong and Songpan (see p204). The airport is located 30 mins by taxi from the city centre (60RMB).

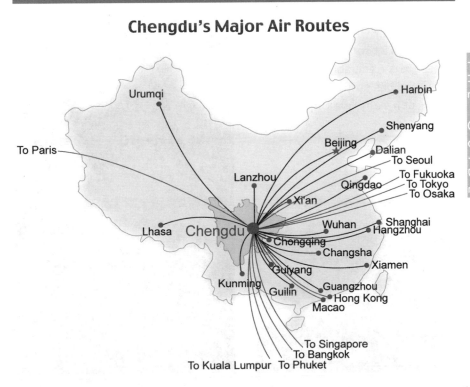

Chengdu's Major Air Routes

Train

Two train stations serve Chengdu, the North Railway Station (Huochebeizhan 火车北站) and the South Railway Station (Huochenanzhan 火车南站). Tickets can be hard to come by and you need to go to the station to buy them in advance. An easier option is to ask at your hotel or hostel reception as they often offer booking services (for a small fee). Trains leave daily for Yibin (50RMB/8 hours), Zigong (40RMB/6 hours) and Emei town (22RMB/2 hours) within Sichuan, and Kunming (240RMB/18 hours), Chongqing (65RMB/4.5 hours), Beijing (420RMB/26 hours) and Xi'an (220RMB/18 hours). Within Sichuan buses are considerably quicker than trains and bus stations are located more centrally making access easier.

Bus

Buses are probably the best way to get to other parts of Sichuan province, particularly due to the recently constructed highways that now serve Chengdu. Fast, smooth expressways now head to the top tourist destinations around Chengdu and make daytrips to sights such as Emei Shan and the Dujianyuan Irrigation System extremely easy. Chengdu has a whopping nine bus stations but the vast majority of tourist destinations are served by buses leaving the Tourist Transport Centre (Xinnanmen Bus Station 新南门车站). The station has a comprehensive English timetable just inside the main entrance (non-existent in other parts of the province) making travel easy and convenient. Buses leave every 20 mins to Emei (35RMB/2 hours) and Leshan (30RMB/2 hours), every half an hour to Dujiangyan (17RMB/1 hours), every hour to Kangding (120RMB/8 hours) and twice daily to Yibin (95RMB/4hours). Buses to northern destinations generally leave from Chadianzi Bus Station茶店子汽车站. There are 4 daily buses to Jiuzhaigou (90RMB/12 hours), 3 daily buses to Songpan (50RMB/8 hours) and a daily departure to Wolong (20RMB/4 hours – dependent on road conditions).

Taxi

Compared to most of China's other cities, hailing a taxi, especially during rush hours, can be a long and frustrating process in Chengdu. It is best to avoid trying to get across town during peak times and a lot of the times hopping on a pedicab or walking is the quickest option. It is easier to hail a taxi from outside larger hotels than off the street during these busy times. Taxis are however clean, reasonably priced (starting fare 6RMB) and honest. It is always best to have your destination written in Chinese as taxi drivers seldom speak English, let alone read it. Taxis to the airport generally charge around 60RMB including toll fares.

Discover Chengdu

Wenshu Temple

文殊院

15 Wenshuyuan Street ⊕ open daily 08.00-18.00; ¥ 10RMB.

Located down the charming little Wenshuyuan Street is a beautifully preserved Buddhist temple complex. Originally called Xinxiang Temple, it was built during the Tang Dynasty and renamed many years later in 1681. According to legend, a monk named Cidu came to the temple and lived in small hut for many years. Upon his death and cremation, the image of Wenshu (Bodhisattva Manjusri) appeared in the flames. From that day onwards, the temple became known as Wenshu Temple and today the large brown tourism sign outside reads 'Manjusri Temple' as it is still often referred to by this name.

Tang and Song Dynasty cultural relics form the heart of the temple which is comprised of many elaborately decorated halls. Paintings, artwork, handwritten texts and calligraphy pieces are all on display. To the many Buddhist worshippers who come to pray, perhaps the most important relic is a piece of broken skull belonging to Xuan Zang, a renowned Tang Dynasty monk.

A vegetarian restaurant inside one of the temple halls offers traditional meat-free Buddhist dishes and full banquets can be ordered for between 200-700RMB.

Du Fu's Thatched Cottage

杜甫草堂

🕐 *open daily 07:00-19:00,* ¥ *60RMB*

Set in the beautiful 24-acre Huanhuaxi (Flower-rinsing Creek) Park, Du Fu's Thatched Cottage is many things – a memorial, a site of extreme beauty, and a haven from the manic rush that is such a part of life in Chengdu. Du Fu's Thatched Cottage is located in the western part of Chengdu on Qinghua Lu, amidst a large park full of museums and statues dedicated to Chinese poets through the ages. The south gate of the cottage opens out into Huanhuaxi Park.

The Story So Far

In 759, during the prime years of the Tang Dynasty, China was being ripped apart by the An Lushan Rebellion. This was when the poet Du Fu, at this time still something of an unknown, arrived in Chengdu. Having been displaced from several homes due to the events of the re-bellion and the pressures of work-ing in the Emperor's court, Du Fu sought a place of peace and refuge. He built his legendary thatched cot-tage on the present site some time around 760.

Du Fu lived in Chengdu for about four years, after which he left to return home to Luoyang. His thatched cottage remained stand-ing until it was destroyed some time in the 9th century. It wasn't until the

16th century that the Emperor Hongzhi of the Ming Dynasty or-dered the cottage to be rebuilt. Us-ing descriptions of the building con-tained in Du Fu's poems, the cot-tage was rebuilt on the site where it now stands.

The cottage was renovated in 1997, and many of the exhibits and buildings in the park were retouched at the same time.

Huanhuaxi Park

This delightful little park is resplendent with landscaped pathways, serene waterways and statues. A neat little aspect of Huanhuaxi Park is the collection of various dioramas set around the park, designed purposefully to provide artists and poets with inspiration. 'The House near a Creek and a Bridge', and the 'Boat Abandoned Motionless in a Lonely Creek' are both worth seeking out.

Alternatively, take a stroll along Huanhuaxi, the creek that gives the park its name. Both the creek and park are named after Lady Huan Hua, a Tang Dynasty noblewoman who saved Chengdu by raising, financing and leading an army of militia to protect the city from bandits whilst the regular army was away with the Emperor in Chang'sha. The creek runs to the south of Du Fu's Cottage, through groves of willow and blossoming trees and into a small lake.

The park is a hive of gentle activity. University students come here to study and take advantage of the tranquility, couples stroll by arm in arm, Chinese teenagers take endless photographs of themselves with the countless statues and beautiful flora, and the older generation comes here to practice tai chi, write poetry, or just sleep in the afternoon sun. It's the ideal place to come to get away from the rigours of the city, especially if you want a relaxing morning or afternoon after more exhausting sightseeing.

Du Fu's Thatched Cottage Park

Locked away from the hustle and bustle of Chengdu by a large terracotta wall, Du Fu's Thatched Cottage Park is a 300ha complex containing not only the poet's home, but also a series of pavilions, an art gallery, a hall with statues and information about China's most famous poets, and one of the most famous photographs of Chairman Mao ever taken.

Strolling through the large wooden gates into the park, the whole world seems to change. The sounds of the city outside are replaced by the chirping of songbirds and the hushed tones of reverence as Du Fu fans and scholars stroll through the shady groves of gingko and hibiscus trees.

Gates containing statues of Du Fu and some of his contemporaries line the pathways, and eventually lead to the cottage itself. Standing in a shaded clearing, it exudes an understated majesty that belies the materials used in its construction- the walls are made of simple plaster-and-wood construction, and the roof is thatched in a style complicit with the Ming dynasty. Open wall panels allow access to Du Fu's study, bedroom, and kitchen.

After leaving the cottage, take a stroll down the legendary Garden Path, immortalised by Du Fu when he wrote the lines 'the garden path has never been cleared for the visit of a guest' in a poem about his house. To your left is a shrine to Lady Huan Hua, and round the corner at the end of the path you will find a large mosaic of two Chinese characters that simply read 'Cao Tang', or Thatched Cottage.

It is not uncommon to spot Chinese visitors having their photographs

taken here in a distinct pose – hands clasped at the small of the back, head tilted slightly to the left while reading the characters. A small black-and-white photograph on the wall here explains why; as during a visit to the park in 1958, Mao Zedong was snapped admiring the mosaics and the photograph was published – the first time his back had ever been caught on film and displayed in public. Nowadays visitors like to emulate this famous pose - to varying degrees of success.

On the Road

Simply tell any taxi or pedicab driver to take you to 'Du Fu Cao Tang' (12RMB/10RMB) and sit back and enjoy the ride. Bus numbers 17, 35, 82, 84, 301, 309, 503, and 509 stop opposite the park on the way out of the city centre.

Chengdu Giant Panda Breeding Centre

成都大熊猫繁育中心

Tel: 028-83516748; @ www.panda.org.cn;
email: pandaivf@mail.sc.cninfo.net; ⏰ open daily 08.00-18.00; ¥ 40RMB

Located 10km from downtown Chengdu, the breeding centre is a surprising natural haven in the midst of a big city. It is easy to forget that minutes away the hustle and bustle of Chengdu pumps on regardless

whilst within these grounds, pandas thrive in their big enclosures, munching contentedly on bamboo, oblivious to the delighted visitors who come to see them. The park is beautiful, with small bamboo tunnels forming paths that weave their way round the sprawling grounds. A large man-made lake is home to 90 different species of birds including white and black swans, Black-

necked storks, wild geese and peacocks. Enclosures have been designed and constructed with the animals' comfort and quality of life considered above all else, and dense trees and vegetation allow them to hide away from the glare of the cameras for a bit of privacy.

While the obvious and justified main attractions are the giant pandas, the red panda enclosures should definitely not be missed. The red pandas are as cheeky as the giant ones are laid-back and charge around their enclosures playing and getting up to mischief.

THE GUIDE

The breeding centre is revolutionary with respect to the study and conservation of Sichuan's indigenous and world-famous giant panda. International cooperation with science units, colleges and universities has helped to bring the work of the research centre into the international limelight and help improve the already outstanding work being carried out. The centre was opened in 1987 and covered just 5.5ha. Today the vast park is under constant expansion, with plans to drastically extend it now under way.

Scientific studies on the critically endangered giant panda cover topics such as biology, reproduction, genetics, disease control, nutrition and behavioural studies and the centre has been awarded 48 national and international awards for its work over the years.

Apart from the adult panda enclosures, visitors can also visit the nursery where live video streams broadcast images of mothers and babies. A fascinating (if somewhat graphic) video has regular showings and depicts the complex and delicate process of panda reproduction and birth. The museum is best visited only if you have some time to kill as the rest of the park is considerably more interesting.

Considering its immense popularity, the research centre doesn't feel crowded or noisy. Getting there at 8am is highly recommended as it will be just you and the pandas – bigger tours don't arrive until after 9am. Small electric buses silently ferry people around the park, but walking around the beautiful grounds is one of the main attractions and highly recommended.

On the Road

The easiest way to reach the centre is to book yourself onto a tour (70RMB including entry) that will pick you up from your hotel and drop you off there later. Most hotels and hostels organise their own trips so ask at your reception. Getting there by public transport isn't easy unless you take a taxi (40RMB each way). Buses from Qinglongchang Bus Station 青龙场汽车站 heading to Longtansi will drop you off outside the centre.

Yongling Tomb

王建墓

¥ 10RMB.

The Yongling Tomb is the Royal Tomb of the Emperor Wang Jian, who is remembered and revered for founding the Former Shu kingdom which followed the collapse of the Tang Dynasty. Under his control, the Shu Kingdom controlled most of Sichuan as well as parts of Gansu, Shaanxi, and Hubei.

Wang Jian's tomb is one of the must-sees on a trip to the city. Famous for its detailed carvings displaying Buddhist and Taoist styles, its most famous feature is a carving of the emperor himself as well as twenty-four Court Musicians and twelve Hercules that decorate the huge burial platform. A small museum (in Chinese only) displays some of the rich finds unearthed from his tomb.

People's Park

人民公园

Located just to the southwest of the city centre, People's Park (Renmin Gongyuan) is a bustling, lively place to spend a few hours. It is the busiest of the city's major parks, popular with both old and young, and features an underground fun house built into an old air raid shelter and a teahouse famous throughout China.

The centre piece of the park, towering above the bonsai trees and perennials that line the paved avenues, is the Monument to the Martyrs of the Railway Protection Movement. In 1911, a band of civilians rose up against the Qing government's plans to remove the Yuehan and Chuanhan railways from civilian use. Through August and September, several strikes and protests were held throughout Sichuan and other provinces.

The leaders of the movement were arrested, and this prompted a massive demonstration outside the Governer's office. On September 7th, 1911 Governor Zhao Erfeng ordered his troops to fire on the protesters, killing 32 of them. These opening gunshots signalled the start of the Wuhan Uprising, which eventually led to the overthrow of the Qing Dynasty and the start of the Republic.

Nearly 100 years later, and the park seems a million miles removed from the gunfire and turmoil that precipi-

tated its creation. Like most other parks in China, a walk through Renmin Gongyuan is the perfect chance to see the residents of the city at rest and play. Dance classes, mahjongg and card games, tai chi practice and nap-taking are common practice here, the practitioners seeking secluded spots away from the raucous children or public events and ceremonies that take place almost daily in the park's main square.

The People's Teahouse

People's Park's very own teahouse is among the best in the city, if not the province. Although often quite busy, it is the perfect place to sit and while away the hours. Not only is the tea absolutely fabulous, the people-watching potential of the teahouse is enormous. In fact, the relationship between the park and the teahouse is almost completely synonymous - one Chengdu resident quipped that "To come to People's Park and not have a cup of tea is almost unthinkable."

On the Road

Ask a taxi or pedicab driver to take you to Renmin Gongyuan (6RMB/4RMB from city centre). Prepare to haggle hard, though as pedicab drivers will try and get 10rmb off you during peak periods.

Sichuan Opera

¥120RMB/person excluding dinner; shows start at 20.00.

The Sichuan Opera is one of the city's most famous and well-loved arts. Unlike many of China's more serious operatic shows, the Sichuan opera is light-hearted, humorous and thoroughly entertaining. Shows generally follow a slap-up meal in a large, raucous dining hall, designed to reflect those of ancient times.

Opera arrived in Sichuan around the end of the Ming and beginning of the Qing dynasties with the influx of immigrants from all over the country. People from different areas brought different styles, dialects, customs, music and dances which combined to form the unique flavour that is the Sichuan opera.

In contrast to the traditional face-painting that characterises much

Chinese opera, most notably the Beijing opera, the Sichuan style uses masks. While a show comprises many different sketches, the most famous and popular are the extremely impressive mask changing scenes. Actors can change masks up to ten times in less than 20 seconds at a speed invisible to the audience's eye. A rapid swishing motion over the face results in an instantaneous expression change, where colours reflect the emotions of the character (sometimes even Spiderman appears, much to the crowd's delight!).

In addition to the mask changing scenes, which often appear as a much-anticipated finale, a whole host of short scenes are acted out, providing a taste of what, during its heyday, would have been hours of entertainment. Girls wearing rainbow-coloured costumes dance in sychronisation, long peacock feathers atop their heads adding to the grace of their delicate movements, while magicians rile the crowd with their tricks and gimmicks. Tea-pouring ceremonies, a hand shadow puppet show and fire spitting are just some of the sketches included in an hour-long show.

Aside from the mask changing, one of the most impressive sketches is that of an erhu solo. The erhu is a traditional Chinese musical instrument comprised of one string. It is often referred to as the 'Chinese violin' and is reputedly extremely difficult to master. Talented musicians play several pieces in an opera show and are certainly one of the highlights.

With a repertoire of thousands of plays, Sichuan opera is reputed to have over 3000 stories from the Tang Dynasty, 800 from the Song Dynasty and an endless number of Three Kingdom tales. Most characters in the wider repertoire have been adapted from Chinese novels, legends, mythology and folk stories. One of the key elements of Sichuan opera which makes it so appealing is its humour. Sichuan women are well-known for being tough with their unruly husbands, and humorous sketches of 'soft-eared' men performing tricks to appease their womenfolk cause much audience hilarity.

Countless venues all over the city have regular shows so it is best to ask at your hotel or hostel to book you tickets (tickets at weekends are more difficult to come by so it is recommended to book ahead).

Emei Shan

Emei Shan 峨眉山

🕐 *open daily 08.00-22.00,* ¥*120RMB/two days*

𝒜bout 160km southwest of Chengdu, towering over the nearby town of Baoguo, lies the majestic Mount Emei. One of the four Sacred Buddhist Mountains of China (the others being Mount Putuo, Mount Wutai, and Mount Jiuhua), Mount Emei is one of Sichuan's largest and most famous attractions. Listed as an UNESCO World Heritage Sight, it is a wonderful place to visit if you want a dose of Chinese culture and the chance to see some fantastic natural scenery.

The Lie of the Land

Mount Emei is actually a range of four mountain peaks. The most famous is the twin-peaked Da'e Shan, and it is the eyebrow-like curves of this peak that give the mountain its name (Mount Emei literally translates as 'eyebrow mountain'). Most of the monasteries and popular scenic spots are located here, and it is here that the hordes of Chinese tourists can be found during the peak season.

The range totals 23km in length, running from north to south. Covering a total area of 115sq km, the mountain and surrounding countryside boasts lofty forests of fir, pine, and cedar, imposing crags stretching into the clouds, and swift-flowing rivers of crystal-clear mountain spring water. All of these are passed on the way up to the mountain's highest point – the Wanfo (Ten Thousand Buddhas) Summit, which peaks at an impressive 3,100m above sea level.

The initial entrance into the park can be confusing, so try this method: buy a half-way bus ticket, and take the bus from the bus station behind the ticket office to Wannian Bus Station. You can only buy entrance tickets into the park proper from the Baoguo, Wuxiangang and Wannian bus stations, so don't worry about not having a ticket just yet.

The Story So Far

People have lived in the region around Mount Emei since the Warring States period, when the area was ruled by a series of warlords and different city states. However, the mountain itself didn't really begin to develop until Buddhism arrived in the area in the first century BC.

The mountain had been an important Taoist centre up until then, and according to legend the Taoist master Tian Zhenhuangren achieved immortality while meditating on the mountain slopes. However, after the Buddha Samantabhadra preached a sermon to 3,000 of his disciples on the slopes of Mount Emei, temples began to flourish on the slopes of the mountain, and its reputation as a centre of Buddhist worship began to spread.

At one point, over 100 temples and places of worship dotted the slopes of Mount Emei. However, due to the ravages of time, war with the Japanese, and the Cultural Revolution, many of these places were destroyed or damaged beyond repair. Since the 1980s, the Chinese government has launched a massive effort to preserve Mount Emei as a centre for both tourism and religious worship, and in recognition of these efforts Mount Emei was added to the UNESCO World Natural and Cultural Heritage List on December 6, 1996.

Walking the Trail

There are a dozen different ways to ascend the mountain, but the most popular trail runs as follows: start off at Baoguo Temple (Declare Nation Temple) at the entrance to the mountain and take a bus to Wannian Bus Station. From there stroll up a fairly steep climb (helped by the availability of a cable car from the start to the halfway mark) to the Long Life Monastery. The oldest monastery on Mount Emei, the monks of Long Life are custodians of one of the mountain's greatest treasures – an 8m high statue of Samantabhadra riding an elephant, crafted in bronze and copper.

From here, continue heading north past a jumble of small temples, and head through one of the many macaque monkey reserves on the mountain as you make your way to Elephant Bathing Pool. According to legend, Samantabhadra brought his elephant here to bathe in the spring water. Nowadays, pilgrims and trekkers alike hang out here, as it marks the convergence of the two major trails up the lower half of the mountain.

From here, the last leg up the mountain takes you up to Golden Summit Temple, the highlight of the trip for many people due to its amazing atmospheric phenomena and views of the Sea Of Clouds, and legendary sunrise and sunset views. Here, if you're incredibly lucky, you may get to witness 'Buddha's Aurora', rainbow-coloured lights dancing around the shadows cast by both buildings and tourists.

If you desperately want to get to Wanfo Temple, there is a monorail (50RMB return) that zips between the two peaks.

If not, then it's time to start the climb down: this time, head south from Elephant Bathing Pool to take in the Magic Peak Monastery, Joking Monkey Area, and the aquatic peace and quiet of Qingyin Pavilion. This area is renowned as being the most scenically beautiful on the entire mountain, and is populated in several places by the ever-present macaques.

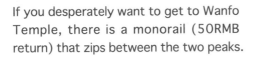

Monkey Business

An integral part of the trip is passing through one of the many macaque monkey reserves that dot the trail. The monkeys have been here as long as anyone can remember, and have formed a harmonious co-habitation with the monks and tourists. They are completely at home around people, a fact that they have developed into a singular talent: thievery.

The monkeys have many techniques for wheedling food from unsuspecting visitors – sometimes blocking the path, demanding food for passage. Many a tourist has been surprised by a monkey dashing from the undergrowth or

from under a bridge to steal a treat from a backpack, pocket, or hand. Keep all fizzy drinks, sweets, and fruit under lock and key – these monkeys have a passion for sugary goodies. So much so that bottles of water and tea are ignored in favour of an obsession with Sprite and Coca Cola.

Duration

The entire trek, based on walking from Wannian to Golden Summit Temple and back down to Baoguo Temple, can be done in two days. However, this is dependent on the number of visitors and the weather. If you do want to get it over with this quickly, be prepared to trek for at least ten hours a day, and to put on a hell of a pace. Those who aren't that crazy, budget three days to do the whole lot.

Accommodation

There are hundreds of guesthouses dotted along the route, all of which offer reasonable rates and basic rooms. The monasteries themselves often offer the best accommodation, and range from 20RMB to 150RMB per night. Baoguo village at the base of Mount Emei also has several hotels on offer.

Crash out

Teddy Bear Cafe & Hotel玩具熊酒店 *43 Baoguo Lu* 报国路43号; *Tel: 0833-5590138; 35RMB/dorm, 80-150RMB.* The Teddy Bear offers great cheap food, and comfortable rooms. Andy the owner speaks great English, knows everything there is to know about Emei Shan, and can give hints and pointers on what to see. Be sure to talk to him before setting out.

Splash out

Hongzhushan Hotel红珠山大酒店 *Tel: 0833-5525888; 350RMB/double.* Well located at the base of the mountain in Baoguo village, this more plush option offers wonderfully equipped rooms and great service. A hearty breakfast is a good start to a long day of trekking.

On the Road

There are two easy ways to get to Emei Shan from Chengdu; by road, or by rail. Taxis to Emei Shan can be negotiated for around 150-200RMB, but the best bet is to take one of the hundreds of buses that leave Xinnanmen Station daily between 06:40 and 19:20 every day. However, be advised that these only take you as far as Emei Town; to get to the mountain requires either a 20RMB cab ride, or taking bus number 1 and changing to bus number 5 after the first stop. Buses back to Chengdu leave every 10 mins from the mountain, with the last bus setting off at 19:00.

To get to Emei Shan by rail, grab the Chengdu-Kunming train from the South Train Station, and simply hop off at Emei Town. Call Andy at the Teddy Bear Hotel and Cafe, or ask at any hostel in Chengdu for train times and prices.

Leshan is a short taxi or bus ride away (30 mins) and buses leave every few minutes throughout the day from the bus station at the base of the mountain.

N

Chengdu 成都市

双流机场
Shuangliu Airport

Leshan
乐山市
峨眉山
Emei Shan

N

万佛顶 Wanfoding

Qianfoding 千佛顶

华藏寺
Huazang Temple
Sheshenya 舍身崖

卧云庵 Woyunan and Golden Summit Temple
太子坪 Taiziping

Cable Car

梳妆台 Shuzhuangtai
接引殿 Jieyindian

雷洞坪 Leidongping

Elephant Bathing Pool 洗象池

华严顶 Huayanding
猴山 Monkey Hill

Jiulaodong 九老洞

仙峰寺 Xianfeng Temple

初殿 Chudian

Magic Peak Monastery

Chapengzi 茶棚子

九岭岗
Jiulinggang

长老坪 Zhanglaoping

Tianchifeng 天池峰

遇仙寺
Yuxian Temple

息心所 Xixinsuo

Hongchunping 洪椿坪

万年寺 Wannian Temple

万年索道 Wannian Cable Car
万年寺停车场 Wannian Park

Niuxin Temple 牛心寺

Chunyangdian 纯阳殿

Zhongfeng Temple
中峰寺

白龙洞 Bailongdong

Leiyin Temple
雷音寺

广福寺 Guangfu Temple

神水阁 Shenshuige

伏虎寺
Fuhu Temple

报国寺 Baoguo Temple

至峨眉山市区 To Emei Shan town

T H E   G U I D E

169

Leshan

Leshan 乐山

0833-2302702; 07.30-19.30 May – Sep, 08.00-18.00 Oct-Apr; ¥ 70RMB entry/50RMB boat tour

*F*amed as being one of the world's biggest stone statues of Buddha, the Leshan Giant Buddha (or Da Fo) really has to be seen to grasp its sheer enormity. Rising 71m from his feet to the tip of his head, the Giant Buddha stands guard over the tempestuous confluence of the three rivers that meet below him.

The Story So Far

Leshan sits on the threshold of the meeting of three raging rivers, the Min, Qingyi and Dadu Rivers. Throughout history, the violent waters have claimed the lives of many who lived in the region and made their livings from the churning waters. Concerned for the safety of the people, a monk named Hai Tong was inspired to create a giant Maitreya Bodhisattva (Future Buddha) to tame the water spirit blamed for the deaths. It took Hai Tong 20 years to raise the money needed to begin such a construction, which began in 713 in the Tang Dynasty and took 90 years to complete.

The Giant Buddha

Imagine a 3m long eye staring back at you and you can begin to comprehend the size of the statue and the colossal task it would have been to construct it at a time when cranes and modern machinery were non-existent. Architecturally and decoratively the Buddha is fascinating. 1,021 neat buns cover his head, while the huge-lobed ears were carved out of wood and affixed to the statue with great precision and difficulty. A complex and highly efficient drainage system to direct water away from the statue's body was constructed in the Tang Dynasty and has been preserved until today.

From the main entrance a short 10 min walk will bring you to the tip of the Buddha's head where you can look down the length of his huge body to the rivers below. This is the best place to get up close to the head and face and appreciate the design and detail with which he was created. To the Buddha's right, the Jiuqu Zhandao (Path of Nine Switchbacks) leads down a tight, winding vertical staircase to the base of the statue. Incense sticks burn next to toes the length of a human and it is a dizzying sight to look upwards, taking in the length of his body. Note that what goes down must also come back up and it is a rather hefty 15 min hike up the cliff on the opposite side.

Boat Tours

Boat tours (50RMB) can be purchased from the main entrance and are a great way to see the whole of the Buddha if the weather is clear. Dense fog is unfortunately a common visitor to the area, and it is a waste of time and money to embark on a boat tour if visibility is bad.

On the Road

Buses leave from Chengdu's Xinnanmen Bus Station every half an hour between 07.00 – 19.00 (2 hours/65RMB) and arrive at either Leshan Long Distance Bus Station 乐山长途汽车站 or a bus stop along the main road into town. Taxis or minibuses will take you to the main entrance (15RMB/10mins) or pedicabs can be hired which are a nice way to see some of the town (10-12RMB). Buses back to Chengdu leave from Leshan main entrance every half an hour until 18.00 and from the Long Distance Bus Station every 15mins. Buses to Emei Shan leave every few minutes (7RMB/30mins) and taxis can be hired for 60RMB each way.

Chengdu 成都市

双流机场 ✈
Shuangliu Airport

N

乐山市
Leshan

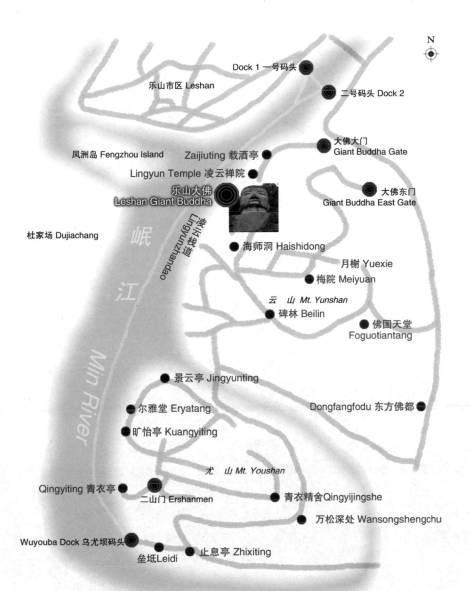

N

Dock 1 一号码头

乐山市区 Leshan

二号码头 Dock 2

大佛大门
Giant Buddha Gate

凤洲岛 Fengzhou Island　　Zaijiuting 载酒亭

Lingyun Temple 凌云禅院

大佛东门
Giant Buddha East Gate

乐山大佛
Leshan Giant Buddha

凌云栈道 Lingyunzhandao

杜家场 Dujiachang

海师洞 Haishidong

月榭 Yuexie

梅院 Meiyuan

云　山 Mt. Yunshan

碑林 Beilin

佛国天堂
Foguotiantang

岷江

Min River

景云亭 Jingyunting

尔雅堂 Eryatang

Dongfangfodu 东方佛都

旷怡亭 Kuangyiting

尤　山 Mt. Youshan

Qingyiting 青衣亭

二山门 Ershanmen

青衣精舍Qingyijingshe

万松深处 Wansongshengchu

Wuyouba Dock 乌尤坝码头

垒坻Leidi

止息亭 Zhixiting

Mount Qingcheng and Dujiangyan Irrigation Project

*A*bout 45km north of Chengdu lies the quiet, unassuming town of Dujiangyan. Not particularly large, or even particularly famous, Dujiangyan nonetheless boasts two of Sichuan's most unique attractions-one a plethora of Taoist culture and history, and the other a testament to Chinese ingenuity and engineering.

Mount Qingcheng

Qingcheng Shan 青城山
🕐 *open daily from 06.00;* ¥ *60RMB*

25km west of Dujiangyan lies the mist-wreathed spire of Qingcheng Shan, one of the five mountains that, in Taoist literature, are responsible for holding the sky above the earth. A much easier climb than Emei Shan, Qingcheng Shan makes for an excellent day trip for anyone looking to get out of Chengdu for a stroll in the country.

Split into two separate mountains, in a range comprising 36 separate peaks, Qingcheng Shan (meaning Azure City Mountain) is a Mecca for Taoist pilgrims and ramblers alike. Taoist history on the mountain dates back thousands of years, to the birth of Taoism as a major belief system (see p74). The ancient Taoist master Zhang Daoling set up the Temple Of The Celestial Master here during the late Han dynasty, the Taoist author and scholar Du Guangting lived and worked here in the 9th century, and more recently, one of Qingcheng Shan's resident monks wrote a piece of music called *Flowing Water,* which found its way into space as part of the Voyager II spacecraft's CD collection.

The first and most popular of the two mountains is Qingchen Shan itself. Loaded with temples and tourist traps, it's the main reason Chinese visitors come to the area. There are two ways to ascend the summit: the first (and most popular) involves taking a ferry across Yuecheng Lake then hopping on to a cable car that brushes the canopy of the trees below, for a gentle 10 min ascent to Shangqing Temple, a few hundred metres below the peak.

The lesser, much more rewarding path follows a winding trail to the east of the mountain, taking you past the minor temples on the route and up a steep path that offers fantastic views of the mountains nearby. The route can be climbed in just over two hours if you're reasonably fit and not particularly bothered about the temples, but to get the best out of this little gem of a mountain spend a few hours taking a leisurely stroll up and back. One word of warning – in places the trail gets very narrow and steep and, while not dangerous, can be a bit slippery in bad weather. Wear good shoes, and take reasonable precautions.

For any student of Taoist history, this trail is a must-see as each temple gives a history and considerable amount of information in both English and Chinese. Although the monks speak little English, if you can speak Chinese (or can find yourself a willing translator) they are more than happy to show you around, philosophise, and tell you stories.

Eventually, you will find yourself at Pengzu Peak, home of the Laojun Pavilion. Named after the Taoist sage and founder Lao Tzu, author of the *Tao Te Ching*, the Pavilion contains a massive multi-storey statue of the sage mounted on a bull. It's an incredible sight, and inspires a real moment of reflection as you catch your breath and give yourself a pat on the back.

The other option for those wanting to get a more natural taste of things, and to avoid the tourist masses, is an overnight hike over the second mountain. Qingcheng Hou Shan (or Back Mountain) offers over 20km of hiking trails that wind through exotic gingko and plum groves, past breathtaking cliff-top vistas, and through quaint little temple complexes and villages at Youyi and Baiyun. Both offer accommodation at around 20RMB per person.

The highlight of the trip is the magnificent Wulong Gou, or Five Dragon Valley. Winding through the towering cliffs and beautiful forests, the trail here offers a marvellous feeling of seclusion, and it was quite possibly here that the poet Du Fu wrote the lines that best encapsulate the atmosphere on the mountain:

"The mountain's secludedness is the greatest under heaven."

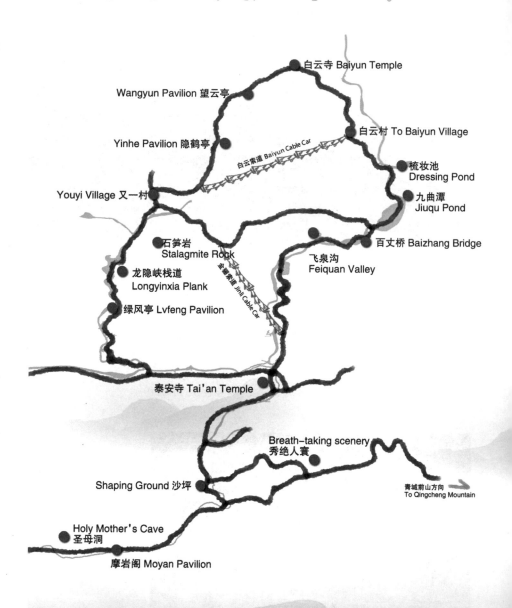

白云寺 Baiyun Temple

Wangyun Pavilion 望云亭

白云村 To Baiyun Village

Yinhe Pavilion 隐鹤亭

梳妆池 Dressing Pond

白云索道 Baiyun Cable Car

九曲潭 Jiuqu Pond

Youyi Village 又一村

石笋岩 Stalagmite Rock

百丈桥 Baizhang Bridge

飞泉沟 Feiquan Valley

龙隐峡栈道 Longyinxia Plank

金骊索道 Jinli Cable Car

绿风亭 Lvfeng Pavilion

泰安寺 Tai'an Temple

Breath-taking scenery 秀绝人寰

Shaping Ground 沙坪

青城前山方向 To Qingcheng Mountain

Holy Mother's Cave 圣母洞

摩岩阁 Moyan Pavilion

Qingcheng Moutain

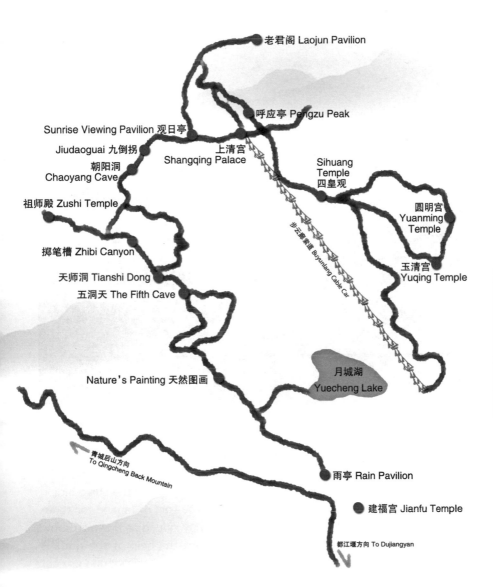

老君阁 Laojun Pavilion

呼应亭 Pengzu Peak

Sunrise Viewing Pavilion 观日亭

Jiudaoguai 九倒拐

上清宫
Shangqing Palace

朝阳洞
Chaoyang Cave

Sihuang
Temple
四皇观

祖师殿 Zushi Temple

圆明宫
Yuanming
Temple

掷笔槽 Zhibi Canyon

玉清宫
Yuqing Temple

天师洞 Tianshi Dong

五洞天 The Fifth Cave

步云廊索道 Buyunlang Cable Car

Nature's Painting 天然图画

月城湖
Yuecheng Lake

青城后山方向
To Qingcheng Back Mountain

雨亭 Rain Pavilion

建福宫 Jianfu Temple

都江堰方向 To Dujiangyan

THE GUIDE

Dujiangyan Irrigation Project

都江堰

🕐 *open daily 06:00-20:00;* ¥ *60RMB*

According to local stories, Chengdu and the surrounding area has not suffered from any sort of famine for thousands of years. Part of this may indeed be down to some sort of divine providence, but the help of the gods is aided to a great extent by the massive irrigation project at Dujiangyan.

In the 3rd century BC Li Bing, Governor of Shu, was caught in a bit of a dilemma. The lack of rainfall and unreliable summer weather meant that crops were variable, and sometimes barely yielded enough food to feed the cities on the Chengdu plain. At other times, the Min River would flood, causing untold damage and death.

So Li Bing and his advisors came up with a bold and ambitious plan: to harness the power of the mighty Min and use it to irrigate the fields and farmlands of the plain.

By digging a series of canals and implementing a genius annual silt-removal programme, Li Bing and his engineers managed to tame the Min and harness it for their own use, without a dam in sight. The project is ongoing and modernising and even though a large part of it has been replaced by unattractive modern dams, it still represents a major breakthrough in the world of water conservancy and to date irrigates over three million hectares of land.

The section of the project open to casual tourism includes the headwork of the irrigation system, and a series of very interesting temples built to honour the engineers and workers who built the original system.

The best way to view this interesting piece of history is to take the number 1 bus to the North Gate and walk down to the South Gate in the middle of town; this avoids the crowds at the entrance and also drops you within feet of a bus stop back to Chengdu.

Highlights include the stomach-churning Anlan Bridge, a 45m chain and plank bridge that crosses the Min River and sways dramatically with each footstep, and the beautiful Lidui Park, at the southern entrance to the project.

It's not the most glamorous place to visit, and the thought of visiting a series of ruddy, murky waterways may put off a lot of visitors, but for anyone with an interest in engineering and water conservation it's a unique and eye-opening experience.

On the Road

Regular buses for Dujiangyan leave Chengdu's Xinnanmen Bus Station every day, between 07:00 and 14:30 (16RMB/1 hour) and terminate at Qingchengshan. To get to the Irrigation Project, take bus number 111 back into town, and ask to switch to bus number 1.

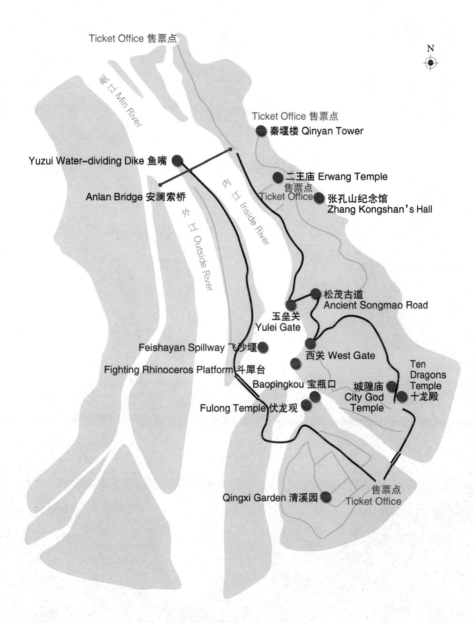

Ticket Office 售票点

N

岷江 Min River

Ticket Office 售票点
秦堰楼 Qinyan Tower

Yuzui Water-diving Dike 鱼嘴

内江 Inside River

二王庙 Erwang Temple
售票点
Ticket Office

Anlan Bridge 安澜索桥

外江 Outside River

张孔山纪念馆
Zhang Kongshan's Hall

松茂古道
Ancient Songmao Road

玉垒关
Yulei Gate

Feishayan Spillway 飞沙堰

西关 West Gate

Fighting Rhinoceros Platform 斗犀台

Baopingkou 宝瓶口

城隍庙
City God
Temple

Ten
Dragons
Temple
十龙殿

Fulong Temple 伏龙观

Qingxi Garden 清溪园

售票点
Ticket Office

Sanxingdui Museum

Sanxingdui Bowuguan 三星堆博物馆

🕒 *open 08:30-17:00;* ¥ *80RMB*

Ask any Western visitor to China what the most archaeologically significant find of the past 50 years has been, and you will almost unanimously receive one answer: the Terracotta Army of Xi'an. Yet on July 18ᵗʰ, 1986, when a group of workmen digging earth for the brick factory in nearby Guanghan unearthed a treasure house of jade and bronze relics, the archaeological community's eyes were opened to a whole new world: the ruins of a vast ancient city dating back to the very beginning of the old Shu kingdom. The ruins were named Sanxingdui, or 'Three-Star Mounds', and they would change the face of Chinese archaeology forever.

Of course, this wasn't the first time that buried treasure had been unearthed in the area; one warm spring day in 1929, a farmer from Guanghan named Yan Daocheng dug up a series of small jade relics while digging an irrigation ditch. However, Yan (not being an archaeologist, after all) gave away most of the trove to family and friends.

The few articles that managed to fall into the hands of academics caused quite a stir, leading to a full-scale archaeological investigation, and over the next few years staff from Huaxi University dug up several hundred items of jade and bronze. A few years, and several hundred artefacts later, the site was abandoned. Until, that is, the 1986 discovery.

Of course, this wasn't the first time that buried treasure had been unearthed in the area; one warm spring day in 1929, a farmer from Guanghan named Yan Daocheng dug up a series of small jade relics while digging an irrigation ditch. However, Yan (not being an archaeologist, after all) gave away most of the trove to family and friends.

The few articles that managed to fall into the hands of academics caused quite a stir, leading to a full-scale archaeological investigation, and over the next few years staff from Huaxi University dug up several hundred items of jade and bronze. A few years and several hundred different artefacts later, the site was abandoned. Until, that is, the 1986 discovery.

Since then, two large burial pits have been excavated, yielding nearly 3,000 gold, bronze and jade artefacts of incredible workmanship. The discovery of the pits caused great excitement among the archaeological community, as the style and craftsmanship of the objects found within are completely different to those of any other period in Chinese history. The discovery of the site essentially had the effect of pushing the perceived date of the Bronze Age in China back by as far as a thousand years.

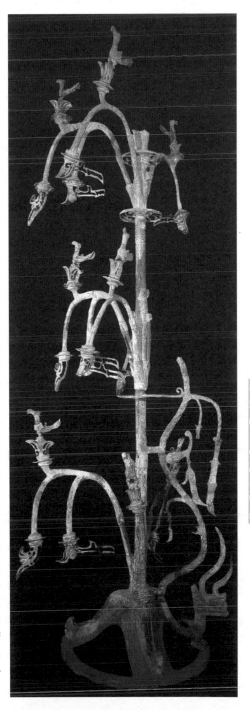

Eventually, through extensive excavations, it became clear that Sanxingdui was a major city. Stretching over three sq km, and with evidence of all sorts of industry from pottery to winemaking, the ruins repeatedly provided evidence of an enigmatic civilisation hitherto unmentioned in any text or record. Some hypothesise that it was the capital of an ancient Shu kingdom, while some say it is all that remains of an advanced people as yet unknown to us.

Nowadays, the work of this ancient and unknown civilisation is housed for public display in the Sanxingdui Archaeological Museum, a vast landscaped complex housing two main museum buildings. The first is an exploration of the tools and practical instruments discovered, from the usual selection of weapons and daggers to articles of religious worship. The most famous of these is a bronze tree, adorned with carvings representing celestial figures such as the sun and moon.

The second hall, as well as containing a massive, 13m tall reproduction of the above tree, is home to Sanxingdui's other famous treasure: a series of masks, wrought in bronze and some inlaid with gold, which line the halls of the building. Darkened lighting doesn't help improve the eerie and often unsettling appearance of the masks, which leer out from inside glass cases. The masks, while obviously representing humans, have vastly exaggerated features; long noses, stretched ears, or even eyes popping out on bronze stalks. Fascinating, but also somewhat unnerving, the Hall of Masks is an interesting glimpse into the world of a mysterious civilisation that, apart from what has been found here, doesn't appear to have ever actually existed.

Guanghan 广汉市
Sanxingdui 三星堆

成都市 Chengdu

双流机场
Shuangliu Airport

On the Road

Buses leave from Chengdu's Zhaojue Bus Station 昭觉寺
汽车站 (10RMB/2 hours) to Guanghan 广汉. From there
catch bus numbers 1 or 6 to Sanxingdui. Taxis from
Guanghan cost around 10-15RMB.

Jinsha Museum

Jinsha Yizhi Bowuguan 金沙遗址博物馆
📞028-87303522; 🕐08:00-18:00; ¥80RMB

Sichuan's second major archaeological site is actually located within the confines of Chengdu's commercial district. In a large park set apart for this very purpose, an ultra-modern museum houses the remains of the city of Jinsha, capital of the Shu kingdom in the later part of the Shang and Western Zhou dynasties (around 500 years after the fall of Sanxingdui).

First discovered by workmen in 2001, the Jinsha ruins soon yielded an amazing treasure trove of objects. More than 1,300 articles have been discovered here, made from jade, copper, bronze, gold, ivory, and bone. Although they bear a few similarities to those found at Sanxingdui, the artefacts here are much more in keeping with traditional ancient Chinese craftsmanship.

The most famous item in the haul is a round disc beaten from gold foil, known as the 'Divine Bird'.Believed to be a representation of the God of the Sun, the disc is based upon an ancient Chinese myth that tells the story of the Golden Bird, an aspect of the Sun God which had one wing and one leg.

The museum that these artefacts now call home is among the best in China. Brand spanking new (it opened in April, 2007), an ultra-modern design and fantastic multimedia displays make the Jinsha museum stand out from the rest by a long shot. Brilliantly laid out, comfortable and airy, and with detailed and informative signage, it is a great place to go to get a glimpse into China's past.

The exhibits are arranged into five gallery halls, each with a different theme. As well as the treasures uncovered from the ruins, there are a whole series of other displays that help visitors really get a feel for how the inhabitants of the city would have lived. All the usual displays are here- scenic dioramas depicting daily life, videos and maps, and everything else one would expect from a museum. Jinsha however, goes one step further, featuring state-of-the-art multimedia displays, a hologram movie of how workers would have fashioned jade and whole, untouched graves on display. Most of the information boards are in English as well as French and Chinese.

The dig site itself is covered by a glass floor, allowing visitors to see the archaeologists at work and to look down into the foundations of the ancient city. Some of the burial pits have been left undisturbed, giving visitors a chance to see them as they would have looked when they were freshly excavated.

In spite of its cultural and archaeological significance, the Jinsha site isn't only for history buffs. The museum has beautiful landscaped grounds that provide a lovely stroll among artwork and sculptures based on relics uncovered from the ruins. As a half-day trip, it's one of the most interesting places in Chengdu, and should be incorporated into any trip to the city.

On the Road

Located on Qingyang Da Dao in northwest Chengdu, the Jinsha ruins are easily reachable from just about anywhere in the city. Bus numbers 5, 7, 82, 83, 96, 111, 311, 401, 502, and 503A all run to within easy walking distance of the site.

N

金沙 Jinsha

Chengdu 成都市
Shuangliu Airport 双流机场

Jiuzhaigou

Jiuzhaigou 九寨沟

📞0837-7739753; @www.jiuzhai.com; 🕒07.00-18.00; ¥ high season120RMB entrance/90RMB bus; low season 80RMB entrance/80RMB bus.

*T*he UNESCO site of Jiuzhaigou Valley is unarguably one of Sichuan's most stunningly beautiful natural gems. Covering a vast 720sq km it is a true plethora of vibrantly coloured lakes, sweeping reed valleys, ferocious waterfalls, pine forests and jagged snow-capped peaks. While the park receives the intense attention of copious amounts of tour groups and buses sweep up and down the valley, its sheer size means you're never far from solitude and quiet.

Jiuzhaigou translates as 'Nine Villages' and refers to the indigenous 'owners' of this staggering landscape, where Tibetan culture and customs have been preserved and nurtured and whose residents continue to live their traditional lives despite the influx of tourism. Most of the villages are off the north-south beaten path that weaves up and down the valley, but can be sought out. Mini

buses from the entrance can be hired for a rather hefty price or a long but rewarding walk from the main entrance will lead you to several of the settlements. The A'ba prefecture, in which Jiuzhaigou sits, is seen as the eastern fringes of the Tibetan culture and has been a centre for the Qiang and Tibetan people for over 500 years. Jiuzhaigou also forms the starting point for one of the Tibetan people's longest pilgrimages to Lhasa. Taking up to three years, devout Buddhists will prostrate their way to Tibet's main city, embarking on the spiritual journey of a lifetime.

The park has such an abundance of natural sights that one day is really not enough to fully appreciate them (unless a day hopping on and off the 'green' buses is what you had in mind). To get the best out of your time it is recommended to take the bus to a good starting point and then get away from the crowds and into the heart of nature with an undemanding and extremely beautiful downhill walk.

Discover Jiuzhaigou

1 – Pandas and Peacocks Take the 'green' bus to Panda Lake 熊猫海 located on the right-hand fork of the mountain road. From here walk downhill through wooded forests and past pouring waterfalls towards the unmistakable 5,600sq m Five-Coloured Lake五花海 (also know as Peacock Lake due to its intense turquoise colour). This is probably the most famous of all Jiuzhaigou's sites and it is easy to see why. From here continue south passing The Golden Bell Lake金铃海 until you reach the Pearl Lake Waterfalls 珍珠滩瀑布. Approximate walking time 2 hours.

2 – The Sound of Nature Take the 'green' bus to the final stop of the left-hand fork where rivers, lakes and waterfalls give way to more remote alpine wilderness. In the high peaks and pine forests of this region of the park, it is easy to walk for hours and not pass another sole. From the Jade-Coloured Lake 五彩池 walk south (slowly, as this area reaches over 4000m above sea level) until reaching the Lower Seasonal Lake 下季节海. This is a great place for wildlife spotting and while the elusive panda is rarely spotted, the endangered Golden Monkey is less shy. Approximate walking time 3 – 4 hours.

3 – The Dragon's Lair For a completely different type of landscape, the lower lying lands at the base of the Jiuzhaigou Valley provide for wonderful, easy trekking amidst reeds, swirling rivers and wide, cascading waterfalls. Start at the Shuzheng Cultural Village 树正寨 and cross the river to the open fields and footpath. From there walk southwards past the 50m wide Shuzheng waterfall and lakes, the sapphire-coloured Lying Dragon Lake 卧龙海 and the Double-dragon Lake 双龙海 until reaching the Reed Lake芦苇海. Small waterside footpaths weave through wide fields of wild grasses that sprawl across the basin. Leading out of the Reed Lake is a stunning turquoise river which, in any season, forms a magnificent sight as it snakes between the metre-high reeds. Approximate walking time 2 hours.

4 – Nuorilang Cascades At the fork that marks the centre of the park be sure to get off the bus and walk the 20mins to the Nuorilang Waterfalls 诺日朗瀑布. Here water surges over a vast U-shaped shelf forming the largest travertine waterfall in the park. In winter, when temperatures plummet to well below zero, the waterfall freezes in its torrential path, forming an enormous ice sculpture – an awe-inspiring sight straight from the Tales of Narnia.

5 – A Path to the Divine Take the first left after entering the ticket barriers, cross the river and follow The Zharu Horse Trail 扎如马道west for approximately 3km. It winds through dense woods and rocks, past orchards, ancient

temples, grassy slopes and cattle towards the foot of the holy Mt. Zhayi Zhaga 扎伊扎嘎神山. On the 15th day of every month on the lunar calendar, Tibetans from all over the region come to pay homage to the mountain. The largest festival held in honour of the Bönpo god Mazi is held here on the 15th May. The Qubu and Qumo springs, considered divine by Tibetans, are located next to the Zharu Waterfall 扎如瀑布 and are often frequented by those wishing to purify their minds and drive out diseases. Be sure to make a stop at the beautiful Zharu Monastery 扎如寺, which forms the centre of Mazi Festival ceremonies and is an important part of religious and cultural life. Finish at the wonderfully hospitable village of Zharu扎如镇 for a true taste of traditional life in the Jiuzhaigou Valley.

Jiuzhaigou Town

One road leads through Jiuzhaigou town so it is impossible to lose your way. The town isn't much to look at, comprising mainly of large, plush hotels and restaurants, but is certainly an accommodating and comfortable place to spend a couple of evenings after a long day in the national park.

Accommodation

There are a whopping 90 hotels in the small town of Jiuzhaigou and 22 of them are three or more starred. Needless to say, prices are fairly high especially during national holidays when booking ahead is an absolute must.

Jiu Tong Binguan 九通宾馆 *Tel: 0837-7739879; 30RMB/dorm, 100RMB/double* This big and rather plain-looking hotel is worth the money mainly for its great location next to the train station and a stone's throw from the park entrance. Rooms are basic and unimaginative but clean and do the job.

Sheraton Jiuzhaigou Resort九寨沟喜来登国际大酒店 *Tel: 0837-7739988; www.sheraton.com/jiuzhaigou* As luxurious and classy as one would expect from the Sheraton chain of 4 * hotels, with just a touch of Tibetan flavour!

On the Road

Chengdu is 240km away and there are several transport options for getting to Jiuzhaigou; opened in 2003, the Jiuhuang Airport 九黄机场 offers between 4 and 10 flights daily depending on the season (45mins/ 900RMB) and is located 88 km from Jiuzhaigou. Shuttle buses leave regularly for Jiuzhaigou (2 hours/45RMB) Alternatively buses leave Chengdu Xinnanmen Bus Station daily (12 hours/ 198RMB). Bus number 102 to Songpan and Wenchuan County leaves Jiuzhaigou bus station at 7. 30am, 12.50pm and 15.00pm daily (3 hours/27RMB).

Jiuzhaigou Valley

N

长海 Long Lake

五彩池 Jade-coloured Lake

熊猫海
Panda Lake

Pearl Lake Waterfalls
珍珠滩瀑布

五花海
Five-Coloured Lake

下季节海
Lower Seasonal Lake

诺日朗瀑布
Nuorilang Waterfalls

金铃海 Golden Bell Lake

树正寨
Shuzheng Cultural Village

Lying Dragon Lake 卧龙海

Double-dragon Lake 双龙海

Reed Lake 芦苇海

Zharu Monastery
扎如寺

九寨沟镇 Jiuzhaigou Town

至黄龙
To Huanglong

汽车站 Bus Station

至松潘 To Songpan

至九寨沟县 To Jiuzhaigou County

Just to Know

1 – Within Jiuzhaigou Scenic Park, 'green' buses hurtle up and down the mountain roads stopping as and when they like. As a general rule, buses are more likely to stop on the way down but be sure to point out to the driver on a map (available free from the ticket office) where you want to get off.

2 – Food within the upper reaches of the park is limited to instant noodles and potato chips so it is advisable to bring along lunch or snacks.

Around Jiuzhaigou

Langzhai Tibetan Village 朗寨藏族村

Located at the northern end of town approximately 15 mins by taxi is the quaint little Tibetan village of Langzhai which is a lovely place to spend an hour or two. Offering a glimpse into undisturbed, traditional village life it oozes character and charm. Residents are shy but exceptionally hospitable and being invited in for a cup of barley tea or wine is not unlikely. On the right as you enter is the village hall which is vibrantly and artistically decorated.

Locals are happy and proud to show it off to the few visitors who stumble upon the village. There is no transport from the village so either ask your taxi driver to wait or try and hitch a ride back into town from the main road.

Huanglong Scenic Park

Huanglong 黄龙

🕒 *open daily 07.00-18.00,* ¥ *110RMB*

As you step off the plane in Chengdu International Airport, photographs of Huanglong's shimmering green, blue and turquoise waters immediately stare back at you. And it is easy to see why photographers and tourists alike are drawn like moths to the unparalleled beauty of this natural formation. Set within Songpan County's mountain scenery, lush green forests engulf the unique limestone rock formations which are internationally renowned as being the World's largest, undamaged karst landscape. As water swishes down the valley into the myriad of pools it is easy to see why the Chinese often refer to Huanglong as 'the fairyland on earth'.

Two paths lead up and down the valley through dense forests on either side, emerging into clearings with fantastic viewing platforms overlooking the calcium pools. A relatively demanding walk to the Five-Colour Ponds at the summit of the park and back again takes approximately 6 hours. Alternatively, a cable car deposits visitors at the intersection of the north and south paths just 20 mins walk from

the Five-Colour Ponds. While the northernmost pools are beautiful, they are often the most crowded. The collection of pools located at approximately the 3000m mark are just as nice and far less busy. This is a good option if you're pushed for time and don't want to pay out for the cable car.

On the Road

Jiuhuang Airport is located 44km's from the Huanglong National Scenic Park and 170km (3 hours) from Jiuzhaigou National Park. Shuttle buses leave regularly to the park (1 hour/22RMB) or mini buses can be hired to take you to Huanglong, wait for the afternoon and continue on to Jiuzhaigou (approximately 800 RMB). Buses from Chengdu's Chadianzi bus station make regular trips (12hours/ 90RMB). Songpan is approximately 60 km away and Chengdu bound buses sometimes stop there (be sure to ask beforehand).

Just to know

1 – Oxygen canisters can help with the uphill walk, especially if you're not acclimatized to the higher altitude (10RMB).

2 – Late in the afternoon the downhill path can get extremely crowded, often shoulder to shoulder. To avoid the surge of people, head down the 'up' path for almost total tranquillity and solitude.

3 – Huanglong is fairly isolated and so there is little to do outside of the park boundary. Half a day is ample to enjoy the park and head on to Jiuzhaigou (2-3 hours) or Songpan (2 hours) which have bigger choices of hotels and restaurants. If you do want to stay near Huanglong, the **Huanglong Grand Hotel**黄龙大酒店 *Tel: 0837-7249666* is a 5* rated establishment located within the park boundary and offers good service and clean, spacious rooms.

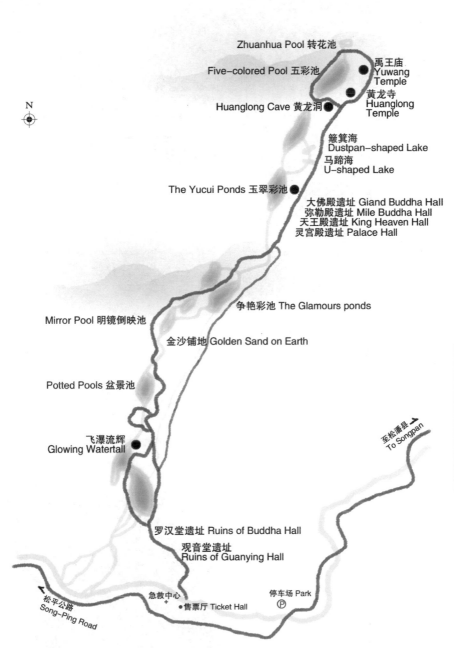

Zhuanhua Pool 转花池

Five-colored Pool 五彩池

禹王庙
Yuwang
Temple

Huanglong Cave 黄龙洞

黄龙寺
Huanglong
Temple

N

簸箕海
Dustpan-shaped Lake
马蹄海
U-shaped Lake

The Yucui Ponds 玉翠彩池

大佛殿遗址 Giand Buddha Hall
弥勒殿遗址 Mile Buddha Hall
天王殿遗址 King Heaven Hall
灵宫殿遗址 Palace Hall

争艳彩池 The Glamours ponds

Mirror Pool 明镜倒映池

金沙铺地 Golden Sand on Earth

Potted Pools 盆景池

飞瀑流辉
Glowing Watertall

至松潘县
To Songpan

罗汉堂遗址 Ruins of Buddha Hall

观音堂遗址
Ruins of Guanying Hall

急救中心
售票厅 Ticket Hall

停车场 Park
P

松平公路
Song-Ping Road

THE GUIDE

Songpan

Songpan 松潘

Located about three-quarters of the way along the route from Chengdu to Jiuzhaigou and Huanglong, the ancient town of Songpan is a great place to spend a few nights on the way to or from the reserves.

The city is located in a beautiful, verdant valley cut by the Min River which now flows through the middle of town. On either side, gentle hills offer some great trekking, and eagles are occasionally spotted soaring above Guanyin Temple, poised high on a hillside on the western side of town.

Songpan grew to prominence during the Tang dynasty, where its location made it a wonderful defensive strongpoint against raiders from the north and west. Huge walls were built, and the entrance to the town was secured by three massive gates. The originals still stand, and form part of the newly-reconstructed city walls.

Today, the town is a hodgepodge of Muslim and Tibetan culture. Within the old city, Tibetan architecture and culture holds sway, while outside the walls the city's mosque towers over streets filled with proud Islamic iconography. The Hui Muslim community here is the largest in Sichuan, stemming from a migration of northern tribesmen during the Tang Dynasty (see p66).

While many come for the famous horse-trekking opportunities, there is, of course, a lot more to this fortress town than just horse riding. Visitors to the town will find that there is a surprising amount to see here. Walking through the streets, you won't find yourself completely overwhelmed by tourist shops – instead Songpan manages to retain a dignified and homely atmosphere, helped by the fact that the myriad Chinese tour buses headed up to the reserves tend to ignore Songpan. This blessing alone makes it a whole lot quieter than many other tourist attractions in China.

As a result, the place is a haven for backpackers, both Chinese and Western. A handful of fantastic hostels (and some not-so-great ones) provide cheap, comfortable accommodation, providing a perfect base to explore the period-style buildings, colourful, friendly streets, and relaxing pavilions and restaurants.

Discover Songpan

Horse Treks

Most people in the West have heard about Songpan for one reason- the legendary horse treks through the surrounding mountains. Horse treks (150RMB/day) run for one to 14 days, longer treks going to Ice Mountain (4 days) or the town of Zoige (12 days). Shun Jiang Horse Treks (顺江旅游马队, Tel: 0837-7231201) offer great service and healthy steeds, and they will help you pick the tour best suited for you. A word of warning- if you're not a Mongol horseman or a full-time rodeo star, expect some serious aches and pains when you stop riding for the day!

City Walls

The city wall walk (40RMB), between the North and West gates, offers a great view of the hustle and bustle in the main streets, past statues of watchmen and warriors in full period regalia. Imaginative visitors may well envision themselves standing in valiant defence of the town against an army of marauding horsemen, while other, nosier individuals may want to sit and watch the townsfolk playing cards or relaxing under the open sky in one of the city's many tea gardens.

Around Songpan

Taoping Ancient Stockaded Village

The village is the best preserved example of Qiang architecture in the province and is certainly worth a detour if you're in the vicinity. The ancient stone block-houses are alive with history, where bright yellow corn-on-the cobs hang from the roofs and wooden walkways weave in and out of the jumble of houses. Arts and crafts, including the famous Qiang embroidery styles, are on display and it is possible to see the people at work making these highly sought after handicrafts. The village is located about 2 hours from Wenchuan between the towns of Songpan and Dujiangyuan. To get to Wenchuan take the early morning bus headed for Chengdu and ask to get off at the town. From there transport to the village is easily found.

Dagu Glacier

Visiting the sprawling Dagu Glacier, especially in winter, is an unexpected and awe-inspiring experience. Located approximately 175km from Songpan in Heishui County, this truly is the heart of Sichuan's northern wilderness. The 30m glacier is considered to be the youngest in the region while the famous Dadu Spring has been declared the oldest. A unique combination of Tibetan and Qiang elements give flavour to the landscape, where sites such as the Selghu Tibetan stockaded village add a personal touch to the abundance of natural resources this region has to offer.

Munigou Valley

The watery landscape of the Munigou Valley is best known for the 104m high Zhagar Waterfall that stretches 35m in width. The water is reputed to cascade over the ridge at a velocity of 23m per second and is a sight to behold. The Erdaohai Valley (meaning two lakes) is named for the Dahaizi and Xiaohaizi lakes and stretches for 5km at the far end of the park. Wooden walkways consisting of a series of planks traverse the narrow valley which contains an abundance of lakes, rivers, caves and lush vegetation. At the far end of the valley a hot spring attracts those in search of its legendary healing properties. Longer horse treks from nearby Songpan often head in this direction.

N

九寨沟 Jiuzhaigou
黄龙
松潘 Huanglong
Songpan

Mianyang 绵阳市

都江堰市 Dujiangyan

双流机场 成都市
Chengdu
Shuangliu Airport

On the Road

Buses to Songpan leave Chengdu Chadianzi Bus Station daily at 06.00, 07.00, and 07:30 (50RMB/8hours). A bus also leaves Jiuzhaigou at 07:20 (3hours/26RMB).

Getting out of Songpan and back to Chengdu can be a nightmare – if you miss the three buses that leave between 6 and 7am, then you can either wait another day, or try and grab a seat on a southbound bus to Maoxian 茂县, then a minibus to Wenchuan 汶川. This is followed by another bus or car ride to Dujiangyan, where, if you're really lucky, you can get a late bus or car headed to Chengdu. In short, be prepared for about 13-15 hours of uncomfortable and stressful travelling.

Just to Know

Emma's Kitchen, just down the road from the bus station, has a great, cheap Western menu. Emma and her brother Dave, speak fantastic English, and are the best people to go to for information on what's going on around town.

Accommodation

There is a whole bundle of budget accommodation in Songpan. Dorms and basic rooms are easy to find.

Crash out

Ice Mountain Hostel 雪山客栈*(Xueshan Kezhan, Shunjiang Beilu); Tel: 0837-8809609; from 20RMB/ dorm)* has friendly staff, clean dorms and shower, and offers laundry service.

Splash out

Songzhou Jiaotong Binguan 松州交通宾馆*(Shunjiang Beilu; Tel: 0837-7231818; 180RMB/double)* has decent rooms- just ignore the none-too-impressive lobby. It's also easy to find built onto the side of the bus station.

Wolong Panda Research Centre

Wolong Xiongmao Yanjiu Zhongxin
卧龙熊猫研究中心
🕐 *open daily 08.00-18.00,* ¥ *30RMB*

*T*he Wolong nature reserve is Sichuan's oldest park dedicated to the protection of the Giant Panda. It was set up in 1963 and in 1980 was designated as a reserve by UNESCO. In addition, the World Wildlife Fund (WWF), whose flagship animal is the Giant Panda, has made considerable contributions and worked closely with Chinese researchers. Covering a vast 200 thousand ha, the park sprawls across the landscape, incorporating towering mountains, dense forests where rare plants and animals thrive, ferocious rivers and jagged canyons. While the main attraction is undoubtedly and understandably the Giant Panda garden, where pandas roll and play, munch the hours away on bamboo and generally melt the hearts of even the most apathetic of visitors, there is much more to see.

Thick, green forests and mountains loom behind the research centre and make for some beautiful hiking, wildlife spotting and bird watching opportunities. **Yingxionggou Valley** 英雄沟 is located approximately 10km north of the park entrance to the left of the Pitiao River. A days trekking will lead you through the dark ancient woods and trickling springs to the mint green of a bamboo sea, the breeding zone of the panda. Jagged cliffs and valley walls, often filled with a dense fog, create an aura of dreamlike and eerie beauty. A kilometre further along the river is the **Yinlong Canyon** 银龙峡. Severe and dramatic, the sharp canyon walls are a beautiful example of nature's power. 11km in the opposite direction, the **Zhenghe Landscape Area** 正河自然保护区 offers a pleasant contrast, with more gently sloping mountain meadows, high rolling peaks and an abundance of flora and fauna. It is best to visit during the spring blossoms but is an extremely pleasant walk most of the year.

The research centre is comprised of several large, leafy enclosures housing a number of pandas of differing ages. One of the most endearing and popular sights are the one year old babies, whose main concerns in life are eating, sleeping and plenty of rough and tumble. Be sure to also pay a quiet visit to the nursery, where tiny infants keep warm inside incubators, and the panda hospital.

Volunteering

Volunteering to help look after the residents of the Wolong Panda Research Centre is, for animal lovers, the experience of a lifetime. While any of the volunteers will happily tell you the majority of time is spent carrying bamboo and cleaning out enclosures, the chance to spend time so close to the animals is enough reward. Opportunities do arise to assist veterinarians, prepare food, observe behaviour and track wild pandas in the reserve as part of the experience. Volunteers sign up for between two days to two weeks and are assigned to a keeper who will keep them busy during their stay. For an extra fee, visitors and volunteers can spend 10 minutes up close and personal with the one year old toddlers who are more than happy to exchange a cuddle for an apple. Accommodation is in the rather nice Panda Inn which is located just outside the entrance to the reserve. For more information visit www.chinagiantpanda.com or www. pandasinternational.org.

Wolong Town

Wolong town is located 7km upstream from the Panda Research Centre. The minute town is just a few hundred metres in length but offers some good, simple eateries, a few small convenience stores and a rather rudimentary internet room - located in a garage behind the building to the left of the Wolong Hotel (2RMB/hour).

Accommodation

Budget option

Tianlong Hotel天龙酒店 *Tel: 0837-8869856; 13154408878; price 80RMB/double* Simple, clean and comfortable, this small, locally-run hotel is the best low-cost option around.

High-end option

Wolong Hotel卧龙大酒店 *Tel: 0837-6246888* This 4* hotel offers lovely spacious rooms, a large bar and café and a hearty breakfast (Western breakfast is available on request for an extra 20RMB).

On the Road

Non-stop buses leave Chengdu Chadianzi Bus Station (3-4 hours/20RMB) regularly. Xiaojin county bound buses leave Chengdu Xinnanmen Bus Station and will drop you at Wolong. At the time of writing the road between Xuankou and Wolong was under construction and transport was limited. Travelling from Songpan, Jiuzhaigou or Huanglong by public transport is arduous and time-consuming, but possible. From Songpan head to Maoxian (3-4 hours/35RMB). From there get on a Wenchuan-bound bus (1 hour/11RMB). In Wenchuan bus station look for minibuses heading to Xuankou 漩口 (2 hours/13RMB) and from there you will need to either stay over and get an early bus to Wolong or hire a minibus (around 600RMB). There are also direct buses from Dujiangyan leaving at 08.00 and 14.00 (3hours/42RMB).

Wolong Panda Research Centre

The Road to Danba

*A*nyone brave – or crazy – enough to try and get to Danba from Wolong is in for a hair-raising ride through some of Sichuan's most treacherous terrain. However, the danger is more than offset by the fantastic sights, views, and feelings of relief that reward those who make it through.

Setting out from Wolong, the road takes you over the forbidding Balang Shan. Nearly 5,000m high, Balang Shan is aptly titled – the name translates from Tibetan as 'Hard Climb Mountain'.

At the time of writing the road over the mountain was still under construction, but should be ready by January 2008, making traversing this stretch of road considerably easier and marginally less terrifying. Driving through the cloud-wreathed pass can be a harrowing experience – trucks bundle down the mountain at ridiculous speeds,

there is a distinct lack of crash barriers over sheer drops, and at times the road is barely wide enough for a bicycle, let alone a minivan. Expect to age a year or two in the five hours it takes to get through the pass, unless you are well acquainted with heights and not bothered too much by drivers speeding up the wrong side of the road. Also, be aware that altitude sickness can hit quite hard during the climb up (see p106).

However, once you hit the peak and begin your descent into the Rilong Valley, be prepared to stop often to take advantage of the amazing photography opportunities. The Rilong Valley is jam-packed with pine trees, Buddhist *stupa*, and mountain views. To the north rise the four snow-capped peaks of Siguniang Shan (Four Girl's Mountain), and you can breathe a sigh of relief as you realise that the hardest part of the trek is over.

Rilong and the Siguniang Mountain Scenery Area

Some 5-6 hours after leaving Wolong, you'll find yourself cruising into the picturesque mountain town of Rilong. Just about large enough to merit 'town' status, Rilong is rather quaint but generally has very little to recommend to most people. For alpinists however, the town provides a fantastic base for climbing, and local guides are credited by the mountaineering organisation K2. Rilong is also home to the Siguniang Mountain Scenery Area, an expanse of mountainous terrain that provides great alpine vistas and some fantastic mountaineering.

Accommodation

Sadly, anyone hoping for a nice comfy Ritz or Hilton after the harrowing haul over Balang Shan is out of luck.

Crash out

Jiarong Hotel 嘉绒大酒店 *Jiarong dajiudian, Tel: 0837-2792888, 120RMB/double* Offers basic but comfortable rooms. Be sure to bring warm clothes as it can get very cold here.

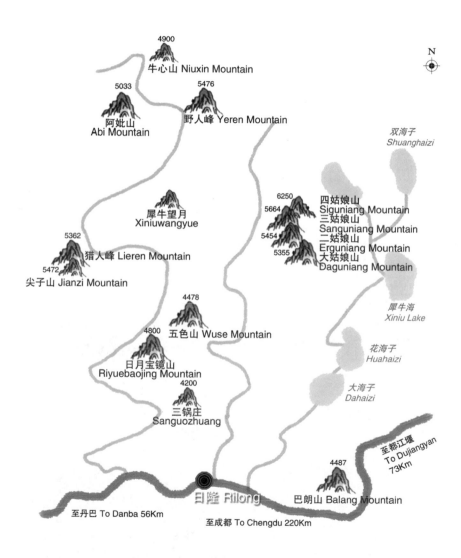

N

4900
牛心山 Niuxin Mountain

5033
阿姙山
Abi Mountain

5476
野人峰 Yeren Mountain

双海子
Shuanghaizi

犀牛望月
Xiniuwangyue

6250
5664
四姑娘山
Siguniang Mountain
三姑娘山
Sanguniang Mountain
5454
二姑娘山
Erguniang Mountain
5355
大姑娘山
Daguniang Mountain

5362
猎人峰 Lieren Mountain

5472
尖子山 Jianzi Mountain

犀牛海
Xiniu Lake

4478
五色山 Wuse Mountain

花海子
Huahaizi

4800
日月宝镜山
Riyuebaojing Mountain

大海子
Dahaizi

4200
三锅庄
Sanguozhuang

至都江堰
To Dujiangyan
73Km

4487
巴朗山 Balang Mountain

日隆 Rilong

至丹巴 To Danba 56Km

至成都 To Chengdu 220Km

Destination Danba

$\mathcal{T}$he second part of the Wolong – Danba route is a comfortable, fairly low-level drive along the Xiaojin River (4hours). As the road follows the twisting course through the valleys it's fairly plain to see how the Xiaojin, or 'small golden river', gets its name – the alluvium silt and sand gives the river a murky, ochre hue. Like many other rivers in Sichuan, the Xiaojin is incredibly fast-flowing, and often broken by large boulders that jut upwards causing massive white-water rapids.

It's a sign of how important the Xiaojin is to the Sichuanese that it gives its name not only to a town (which you will pass through), but also the entire surrounding county. The river is an important part of village and town life in the area, and washerwomen can often be seen scrubbing clothes in the waters while children bathe and old men sit with fishing rod and pipe.

The road passes through several towns of little interest to the casual traveller. Xiaojin is the biggest of these, and a good place to stop and eat, and maybe spend an hour or so strolling around. While not rich in sights, it still has a calm, relaxed atmosphere and some decent restaurants.

Possibly the most singularly impressive sight on the route is the Baotao Monastery, a large lamasery located on the side of a mountain that, according to locals, sits at the far end of a mountain ridge that resembles an elephant bathing in the river. Surrounded by farms perched on terraces carved into the mountainside, the monastery overlooks a treacherously fast bend on the river, watching like a silent sentinel over the small fishing boats that brave the channel.

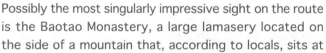

Danba

丹巴

Six hours after leaving Rilong, the road crosses a small bridge, and deposits you in the middle of Danba. A beautiful little town, Danba is cut in half by the Dadu River, and is situated just north of the confluence of the Dadu and Xiaojin rivers. The town itself appears to be built right into the sides of the Dadu valley, indeed some of the town's buildings have no back wall, instead being built into the rock itself.

The main draws of this little gem are the Tibetan and Qiang minority villages that litter the surrounding countryside, many within a day's hiking distance of Danba. Some villages are over 70 years old, though they have all the mod cons- satellite dishes and computers abound in this rustic paradise! The buildings can be distinguished by the four triangular spires topped with quartz on the roof of each, which provide quite a nice glittering display as the sun goes down and its last rays are reflected.

Discover Danba

Zhonglu Village 中路乡

¥ *10RMB*

Located 36km outside of Danba this quaint little village dots the steep slopes of one of the many mountains in this precipitous region. Clusters of ornately decorated farm houses are circled by orchards and terraced fields, animals wander idly up and down the winding, tree-lined roads and villagers go about their daily lives as they have done for hundreds of years. A trip out to the village provides a wonderful insight into the architecture, economy, character and everyday lives of the people who inhabit the area.

Suopo Watchtowers 梭坡古碉群

The other reason Chinese tourists love to visit are the Suopo watchtowers. Located just east of Danba, these incredible little fortifications date as far back as the Warring States period, when villages would build them to watch for enemies, roving raiders, and, of course, each other. In more recent times towers were erected by more affluent members of the communities to commemorate the birth of a son. A rather daunting footbridge swings over the rushing river below and provides access to the village. While this is the best place to see the towers up close (and the setting, perched high above the roaring Dadu River, makes it all the better), watchtowers of differing heights and styles can be found all over the region. Extensive research is being done into these unusual and unique constructions and UNESCO designation is under consideration.

Accommodation

`Crash out`

Zhaxi Zhuokang 扎西卓康青年旅社 *35 Sanchahe Nanlu 岔河南路35号; Tel: 0836-3521806; 50RMB/double* This is a great little place with recently-redone rooms and very friendly staff. The hostel also has its own car, and can arrange trips to the surrounding villages and towers. Just be warned – they don't speak any English here, so picking up a few Chinese phrases will go a long way (see p349).

Wolong 卧龙

Siguniang Mountain 四姑娘山

日隆 Rilong

都江堰市 Dujiangyan

Danba 丹巴

Chengdu 成都市

双流机场 Shuangliu Airport

N

Kangding

Kangding 康定

The city of Kangding forms the gateway to the western fringes of Sichuan province. Located at the threshold of the inhospitable mountain terrains to the west, and the Chengdu basin to the east, it creates not only a physical barrier, but a metaphorical one too. The city is a fascinating and unique mixture of cultures, religions, cuisines and peoples. Stretching for merely a few kilometres in size, Kangding is small and easy to navigate. A main street, about one kilometre in length, follows the roaring river through the city centre upon which a mishmash of shops, restaurants and hotels are located. Modern, six-storey buildings have a definite Tibetan architectural style, while small, run-down wooden buildings house ancient workshops and are a lasting legacy to Kangding's early timber phase. Pricey clothes boutiques dress young Chinese residents in Chengdu's latest fashions, while Buddhist monks sport their traditional red robes and Tibetans complete the eclectic mix with their long dresses and colourful headwear.

Kangding was once used as the wild trading point for Tibetan nomads and Chinese traders who came to exchange yak and sheep skins, handicrafts and barley for manufactured products. It is because of this that Tibetans have always referred to Kangding as 'Dartsedo', or 'meeting place' [of two rivers and of traders]. Today shopping centres exist alongside flourishing markets, the yearly mushroom harvest being one of Kangding's biggest and busiest times.

Discover Kangding

Princess Bridge 文成公主桥

Located 1km outside of Kangding is a lovely little stone bridge built for the Princess Wencheng on her journey to Tibet. It was reconstructed in 1997 and now incorporates intricate carvings of flowers and dragons.

Temples, Monasteries, Mosques and Churches

Kangding is home to a unique and eclectic mix of houses of worship that thrive contently alongside one another. The 17th century **Ngachu Gongpa** monastery is the

largest in the city and used to house over 100 monks. The **Nanwu Lamasery,** belonging to the Geluk sect of Tibetan Buddhism, is Kangding's oldest, its construction directed by the 5th Dalai Lama in 1652 on his journey from Beijing to Tibet. Located on Dongda Jie Street, a **mosque** serves the Hui people who live in its vicinity, and a **Catholic church,** constructed in 1997, is easily identified by its three blue, cross-topped cones poking above the buildings along the main Yanhedong Street.

Racehorse Hill (Paoma Shan 跑马山)

Over-looking the confluence of the Dar and Tse Rivers that characterize Kangding, Racehorse Hill public park is home to the yearly International Paomashan Mountain Fair held on the 8th day of the 4th month on the Chinese calendar (normally 8th April), during which time Kangding is abuzz with festivities and celebrations. A simple Tibetan Buddhist temple sits at the 2700m summit. At any time of the year a walk up the mountain is a pleasant alternative to the hustle and bustle of Kangding.For those with less time (or who are simply not inclined to hike!) a cable car takes visitors to the top (30RMB).

Mugecuo Lake 木格措湖

Not long ago converted into a fully fledged national reserve, this popular lake park is located 26km north of Kangding and is a lovely place to spend the day. It is comprised of huge, forest-bound hot springs and lakes, whose mountain slopes are home to dense forests, blossoming azaleas and the rare Tibetan Gesang flowers. The park also acts as a springboard for a wonderful 1-2 day trek to the town of Tagong (see p278). The trek takes you past the lower slopes of the Zhara Mountain and through sprawling, pristine grasslands.

Zheduo Tang Village 折多山

This quaint little hamlet marks the starting point for one of the area's most popular treks. Believed to be the ancient caravan route for Tibetan nomads and Chinese traders long before the construction of the Sichuan-Tibet highways, a footpath leads to the town of Jiagenba, and takes 2-3 days. Heading out into the wilds of the Tibetan landscape, the trail passes vast grasslands, yak-skin tent settlements, towering mountains, sweeping valleys, roaring rivers and waterfalls and, in the distance, Mount Gongaa's imposing glaciers (see p317).

Accommodation

Kangding is bursting at the seams with hotels and hostels ranging from the sublime to the downright grubby and finding one to suit any pocket is easy.

Crash out

Black Tent Guest House 沿河西路 28 号 *Gonggashan Lushe; 28 Yanhe Xilu; Tel: 0836-8862107; 25RMB/double*. Although outward appearances are a bit shabby this is a top-notch little hostel. Dorms are clean and shared bathrooms are decent. They serve up some great food too; cheap, tasty and lots of it.

Splash out

Love Song Hotel 东大小街156号 *5 Yanhe Donglu; Tel: 0836-2828777; 350RMB/double*. This plush hotel is located right in the middle of the city and offers classy rooms and service rarely seen outside Chengdu. The amount and quality of facilities are impressive, and service is very good.

Just to Know

Kangding is the best (and last) place to buy anything you might need before heading out into the western hinterland of the province. A large supermarket underneath the main square is well stocked and there are small convenience stores everywhere. A couple of camping and hiking stores sell top-notch equipment and clothing if you plan on doing some long treks. Restaurants are scattered everywhere serving Chinese and Tibetan foods and Tibetan tea houses can be found all along the main street. A plush, Western-style coffee house can be sought out up a small alley near the central square (although prices are Western-style too!).

On the Road

Kangding is the transport hub of the east and all buses lead into and out of a rather dishevelled-looking bus station at the far end of town. Most long-distance buses leave early in the morning so it is advisable to buy tickets in advance. Four buses leave for Litang along the South Sichuan-Tibet Highway (see p299) at 6.45am (8 hours/85RMB) and Dege along the North Highway (see p275) at 7am (24 hours/166RMB). The Dege-bound bus stops at Tagong (4 hours/15RMB), Luhuo and Manigange along the way. Buses to Chengdu leave regularly between 06.00 and 16.00 (7 hours/117RMB).

Two types of taxi operate in and around the city. Local, intra-city taxis start at 4RMB and are a convenient way of getting from A to B. At the end of town, a few hundred metres from the bus station, blue, longer-distance taxis will take you to Luding (2hours/25RMB), Zheduo Tang village (30mins/20RMB) or Mugecuo Lake (30mins/ 20RMB) and leave when full. From Luding it is possible to get a minibus to Moxi and the Hailuoguo glacier park.

▲ 折多山 Mt Zheduo
○ 康定 Kangding
雅安 Ya'an
Shuangliu Airport
双流机场
⊕
Chengdu 成都市 ○

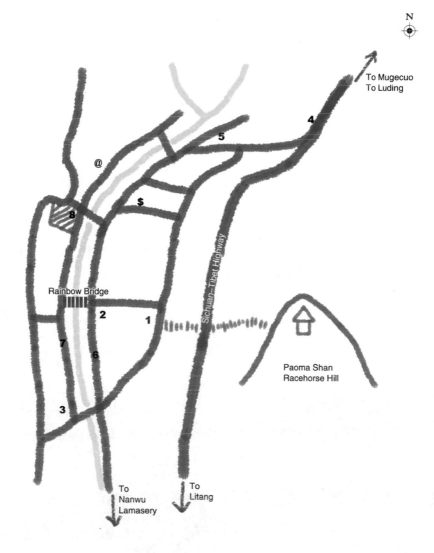

N

To Mugecuo
To Luding

5

4

@

$

8

Sichuan–Tibet Highway

Rainbow Bridge

2

1

7

6

Paoma Shan
Racehorse Hill

3

To
Nanwu
Lamasery

To
Litang

THE GUIDE

1. Mosque

2. Love Song hotel

3. Black Tent hostel

4. Bus Station

5. Blue Long–distance taxi`s

$. Bank

@. Internet

6. Yanhe Donglu

7. Yanhe Xilu

Square

8. Supermarket

Zheduo River

Sichuan-Tibet Highway

Starting at Chengdu and running for 2,413km to Lhasa, the Sichuan-Tibet highway is an impressive feat of road engineering. Begun in 1950, the road took four years to complete. Crossing several peaks of over 6,000m, and winding through the snowy, icy Himalayas, driving the entire route is certainly not a trip for the faint-hearted.

After Kangding, the Highway splits into two roads: the Northern and Southern routes. Both eventually end up in Lhasa, but the environment, sights, and experience of each could not be more unique.

North Sichuan-Tibet Highway

*T*ravelling the more than 2500km to get to Dege and back may seem like a crazy prospect, especially on the notorious northern part of the Sichuan-Tibet highway. Renowned for its permanent state of disrepair, the Northern Route has a maligned reputation as one of the more dangerous stretches of road in China. But for anyone willing to brave the bone-shaking bus rides, icy blasts of wind, and often crude company of the other passengers, the Highway offers a fantastic trip through breathtaking and ever-changing natural scenery.

The route passes through several large towns, and past numerous temples and lamaseries. In fact, the whole northeast Sichuan region is dotted with places of worship, making this an ideal excursion for those with an interest in Eastern religion and philosophy. It is also home to hundreds of nomadic groups, their multitudinous herds of yak, and any number of species of wildlife. In short, there's always something new to see on the trail.

To Jiangzi 至江孜

至日喀则 To Rikaze

N

Lhasa 拉萨

86

75

Dangxiong 当雄

78

Zelan 泽兰

墨竹工卡 Mozhugongka

150

那曲 Naqu

雅鲁藏布江 Yaluzangbu River

Jiacha 加查

206

工布江达 Gongbujiangda

261

48

Milin 米林

19

八一镇 Bayi

巴青 Baqing

Linzhi 林芝

125

236

Tongmai 通麦

89

丁青 Dingqing

Bomi 波密

131

Zhongba 中坝

123

类乌齐 Leiwuqi

Ranwu 然乌

Nu River

怒江

Basu 八宿

86

Bangda 邦达

84

昌都 Changdu

263

澜江 Lan River

109

妥坝 Tuoba

Yanjing 盐井

119

江达 Jiangda

103

111

芒康 Mangkang

Deqin 德钦

金沙江 Jinsha River

111

德格 Dege

179

93

巴塘 Batang

Zhongdian 中甸

171

乡城 Xiangcheng

201

To Dali 至大理

222

112

Daocheng 稻城

148

理塘 Litang

甘孜 Ganzi

137

95

Yajiang 雅江

炉霍 Luhuo

80

71

新都桥

道孚 Daofu

33

Xinduqiao

71

82

Kangding 康定

丹巴 Danba

49

Luding 泸定

62

小金 Xiaojin

163

56

Ya'an 雅安

日隆 Rilong

150

230

成都 Chengdu

THE GUIDE

277

Tagong

塔公

*A*lmost immediately after leaving Kangding, the route turns northwards and climbs steadily through a series of mountain passes, before descending down into the flat plains of the Tagong Grasslands. This wonderful plateau extends for miles in either direction, and is encircled by the rolling peaks of the Himalayan foothills. It's a great place to just kick back and enjoy the early-morning sights, as families in small villages go about their business and the cowboys saddle up for a hard day's work.

The first big sight on the trip comes up roughly five hours after leaving Kangding, as the road winds its way into the sleepy little town of Tagong. A cheerful blend of Tibetan and Han building styles, Tagong is dominated by the Qing-dynasty Tagong Temple, located in the centre of town. There are plenty of little guesthouses around the temple, and several can arrange horse or car trips to the surrounding grasslands.

The best time to hang out in Tagong is during the annual *saimahui* – the world-renowned horse festival, when hundreds of plains folk gather to show off their riding skills and generally have a raucous and lively time.

Leaving Tagong behind, the road climbs up through a series of foothills before opening onto yet another grassy plain. Keep your eyes open for circling birds of prey, including hawks, eagles, and vultures, and cattle-herders marshalling their vast herds of yak across the green vistas. Also, throughout this part of the grasslands, expect to see hundreds of black tents. These are the homes of the nomadic Zhuang people, and are made of wood and dried yak hide.

Accommodation

Crash Out

Snowland Guesthouse雪城旅社 *(XuechengLvshe; Tel: 0836-2866098; from 15RMB/dorm),* is by far the best of the cheap options in town. It is located next door to the temple. The beds are incredibly comfortable and the blankets are the cosiest you'll find west of Chengdu.

Luhuo

炉霍

*A*fter a drive through some incredibly diverse scenery – the plains give way to steep, tree-filled alpine valleys, which in turn fade into a dusty, arid desertscape – the trail rolls into the town of Luhuo. Luhuo is almost solely used as an overnighting point for the bus from Kangding to Dege, and there really isn't a lot to recommend for tourists. For those not already utterly exhausted by the twelve-hour trip, there are a handful of monasteries surrounding the town, and a short stroll through Luhuo's streets will introduce you to this town's incredibly friendly inhabitants, who are always willing to point out where everything is.

Accommodation

As soon as you hop off the bus, you'll be swamped by vendors offering cheap accommodation

Crash Out

20RMB a night will get you a very, very Spartan (chipboard walls, a bed and a TV) room at the bus station. 'Room' may be a touch generous – the 'hostel' has conditions akin to a private version of a migrant worker dormitory. Opposite the bus station is another hostel, offering vaguely cleaner doubles for 40rmb.

Splash Out

Casan Commercial Hotel 卡萨商务酒店 *18 Tuanjie Lu; 160RMB/double* is the best of the lot. Turn right from the bus station, and walk about 100m up hill. It may be a lot pricier than other places but guarantees a warm, vermin-free night's sleep.

Ganzi

甘孜

*T*wo hours past Luhuo, the highway hits the town that is, for many people, the highlight of the trip. Ganzi is a lively, colourful market town of around 60, 000, and the atmosphere here is so laid back, it's practically horizontal. Another valley town, Ganzi is surrounded on all sides by mountain ranges, including Snow Mountain, a white-capped giant that rises to the south west, and Chola Mountain to the northwest.

This fantastic scenery leads many visitors – many of whom just intend to pass through – to stay here for three or four days and take in a hiking tour through the outlying villages. Most hotels can recommend a guide or a route, or you can just as easily set out on your own.

The people of Ganzi are a lively, friendly bunch. A walk through the city's main shopping areas can be a rewarding and enlightening experience. Rapid-fire exchanges in Tibetan are common, and good-natured haggling is the norm. Just beware if you've spent a lot of time learning Mandarin Chinese, as the area around Ganzi is predominantly Tibetan-speaking and you may find yourself talking more in English than Chinese.

Discover Ganzi

Ganzi Temple

Ganzi's biggest, most famous tourist attraction is the massive Ganzi Temple, over 500 years old and home to almost 500 monks. Perched on a hillside overlooking the town, the best way to get here is to take a taxi from the city centre (10RMB but be prepared to haggle as drivers don't often use the meter) then walk back into town through the Tibetan Quarter.

The monks who live here welcome tourists with open arms, and are a very lively and friendly bunch. All are willing to sit and chew the fat (if your Tibetan is good enough), and if you're lucky, you may catch some of them making yak-butter candles, performing rituals, and going about their daily tasks.

The temple is also home to a massive golden statue of Maitreya, the Future Buddha, set in a gorgeous hall designed to both awe and calm those who enter. From the large open galleries to the hundreds of small golden Sakyamuni statues that line the rooms on the second floor, the entire temple radiates an aura of peace and tranquillity, making it very hard to leave.

THE GUIDE

Tibetan Quarter

When you do manage to haul yourself out of the fascinating Ganzi Temple, don't bother taking the main road back to town – a much more pleasant way to get back into the city centre is to head to the northwest corner of the car park, and wander down a flight of hewed-stone steps into the heart of Ganzi's Tibetan Quarter. If you have any trouble, just ask the monks where to go.

The Tibetan Quarter is a quaint mass of sandstone houses, decorated in traditional Tibetan style, and sur-

prisingly untouched by the tourist boom that has taken over the centre of the town. While there's nothing in particular to see here, the quiet streets and the potential for people-watching make this a perfect half-hour stroll, especially if the weather's even remotely nice.

Lamaseries

At the opposite end of town to the Tibetan Quarter are a series of other Lamaseries. Ganzi boasts a total of six, including the Ganzi Temple. The most impressive of these is in fact the seat of the Gyalten Rinpoche. Although he now spends most of his time in Kangding, the Rinpoche works tirelessly to provide the people of Ganzi with various new amenities – a few years ago, he opened a hot springs bathhouse near the monastery, and at the time of writing construction was underway for a community centre for the elderly folk of Ganzi.

Accommodation

Ganzi offers a wealth of decent budget hotels but very little in the way of more upmarket establishments.

Crash Out

Golden Yak Hotel *Jinmaoniu Jiudian*金牦牛酒店, *Dajin Jie*; *Tel: 0836-7522353; 30-180RMB/rooms.* Attached to the bus station, this large complex offers everything from cheap dorms to a great 'A-Class Standard' room which comes equipped with possibly the best showers in Sichuan.

Splash Out

Chengxin Binguan *Dajin Jie* 城心宾馆; *Tel:0836-7525289; from 150RMB/double,* opposite the bus station, offers rooms which are clean and comfortable but basic. Your best bet for a luxury room is still the Golden Yak.

Manigange

马尼干戈

Manigange (or Manigango, to give it its better-known Tibetan name) is certainly an experience. Not really much more than a village, the town consists of a single main street and a few side roads. It is quite undeveloped, and several nice examples of Tibetan architecture dot the main street. Tibetan cowboys (both on horseback and on motorbike) share the street with monks, old women selling trinkets, and vendors offering vast slabs of raw yak meat.

Like Luhuo, Manigange is a stop-off point more than a major destination. Buses headed to and from Dege stop here for about an hour to grab a bite to eat, before continuing onwards. If you do decide to stay for a day or two, the town's two hotels are cheap but not particularly great, and the food choices are somewhat limited.

Discover Manigange

Yihun Lhatso Lake

Manigange is a great place for trekking and the foothills and mountains offer fantastic scenery. The most popular place for travellers to wander out to is Yihun Lhatso, a beautiful glacial lake 13km from Manigange. It is possible to arrange horse trekking throughout the area, but be warned – this can be something of a hit-and-miss enterprise with regards to availability and quality.

Dzongchen Gomp Temple

Of course, it wouldn't be a real Tibetan town without at least one temple of note, and Manigange doesn't disappoint in this regard. An hour's drive to the north, over the chilly Muri La Pass, lies Dzogchen Gompa (Zhuqing Foxueyuan), the home of the Dzogchen school of Tibetan Buddhism. The fact that this school is the most popular form of Tibetan Buddhism in the Western world explains a lot - several of the monks here speak a little English, and pilgrims are a common sight in the small town.

Accommodation

In Manigange, you have a choice of two mediocre hotels:

Crash Out

Manigange Hotel马尼干戈食宿店 *20RMB/single, 25RMB/double* is the spot where all the buses stop, and has doubles for around 25rmb. Beware, though – toilet facilities here are limited.

Splash Out

Yulong Shenhai Binguan玉龙深海宾馆 *30RMB/room* is a little further up the road and is a little more comfortable, and at least has a bathroom.

Cho La Pass

Reaching almost 6,000m in height, Cho La Mountain is a forbidding obstacle as it rises up in front of you. The pass itself is easily visible from the road as it snakes its way up the side of the mountain, a dusty, poorly-constructed highway just wide enough for two buses. Cho La Shan has a reputation for danger and overturned buses, as in bad weather the road can become encrusted with ice. Generally, the pass isn't as terrifying as the guide books make out, especially if you make the trip on a nice day, but it can be fairly nerve-wracking at points.

The biggest danger to watch out for is altitude sickness. It can hit pretty hard up here, as the bus ascends nearly 3000m in a very short space of time. Make sure you come prepared for the worst, and have lots of warm clothes and water – it can get very, very cold on the pass.

If travelling by bus, make sure you're paying attention when you hit the peak. Tibetan passengers on board chant and throw coloured paper out of the window, as the road curls around a large shrine and a series of brightly-coloured prayer flags. Occasionally buses will stop here for a while, so if it does, wrap up warm and get the camera out as the views from up here are phenomenal.

Dege

德格

*A*fter a relaxing drive through alpine gorges and deciduous forests, and past row upon row of prayer flags, this leg of the highway terminates in Dege. At a comfortable 3,200m above sea level, this is the perfect place to spend a few days, especially if you need to recover from a bout of altitude sickness.

A quaint little mountain town, Dege is caught in a transitional period at the moment as modern buildings start to edge out some of the more traditional Tibetan dwellings. Hotels and hostels are springing up at a surprising rate, pilgrims and tourists are coming to the town in ever-greater numbers, and the people here are keen to take advantage of the boom in the town's tourism industry.

Discover Dege

Batong Scripture Lamasery 德格印经院

¥ 40RMB

The main reason for the ever-growing expansion is the world-renowned Batong Scripture Lamasery, a vast, 300 year old storehouse of Tibetan Buddhist writings and one of the largest scripture-producing lamaseries in the world. A vast red-painted temple houses the lamasery, and is constantly circumambulated by pilgrims spinning prayer wheels and chanting in an attempt to complete 1,000 *kora,* or circuits, of the lamasery.

Inside, under the watchful gaze of a large green statue of Avalokiteshvara (known in Chinese as Guanyin), teams of workers produce over 2,500 scripture prints a day. There are no computerised printing presses here – each team comprising of two workers uses a printing rack and a series of printing blocks to reproduce the scriptures on strips of hand-woven cloth.

རྣམ་གྲངས་ཀྱི་རིང་དེ་འཛིན་ལ་སྐྱོབས་པ་རྒྱུགས་སོ། །ཡང་དེའི་ཚེ་
བར་རྣམ་པར་ལྡན་ཏེ། །དེ་ནས་ས་དང་རྒྱུར་ཀྱིལ་ཀྲུས། ཚོར་དཀྱི་
ཕྱིན་པ་ཟབ་མོ་སྲུང་བ་སྲུང་པ་ར་འཛིན་པ་དེས་ི་ལྱར་བསྒྲུབ་པ་ར་ཀྱ།
ས། རྒྱས་ཀྱི་སྐུ་ཚོ་གདལ་ལ་ཤེས་རབ་ཀྱིར་ལྱ་ཧུ་ཕྱིན་ཟབ་མོ་ི
 སོ། །གཟུགས་ལ་མ་སྲོང་བ་འདྲེ་གཉན་ས་ཡིན། སྲོང་བ་རིད་ལས
སོ་དཔ། མ་སྐྱེ་བ། མ་འཁག་ས་པ། རྫས་མེད་པ། དེ་
མེ་གམེ་ད། རྒ་བ་མེ་ད། སྲུ་མེ་ད། ལྷུ་མེ་ད། ལུས་མེ་ད། ཡེང་ཅ

Every other spare inch of space in the lamasery is taken up with storage space for the scripture printing blocks. Thousands of them are kept in shelves and racks throughout the temple, and the latest count puts the total in the region of 300,000. The texts here make up one of the largest libraries of Buddhist scripture in the world, and include several extremely rare books on a variety of subjects.

Other nearby sights include three other lamaseries, one of which is over 1,000 years old, and some fantastic mountaineering and hiking in the surrounding area.

Accommodation

Jiaotong Hotel 交通旅馆 *Tel: 0836-8223819; from 20RMB/dorms*

This is a newly renovated clean, friendly hostel in a great location. The only drawback is that at the time of writing they did not accept solo travellers.

Que'er Mountain Hotel 雀儿山宾馆*Tel: 0836-822167; from 180RMB/room* is the nicest hotel in town. Friendly staff (some of whom speak English), comfy rooms, its 3* rating and a great central location make this the hotel of choice for Chinese tour groups.

South Sichuan-Tibet Highway

$\mathcal{K}$angding acts as the main fork in the Sichuan-Tibet Highway, where the great trunk road splits in two, each finding its own way to the final destination of Lhasa. It is here that the South Sichuan-Tibet Highway begins, veering off the main National Trunk Highway 318 that begins 240km away in Chengdu, and heads directly west into the Tibetan hinterlands and ancient province of Kham. The eight hour journey from Kangding to Litang does, without a doubt, traverse some of Sichuan's most stunning landscapes, the beauty of which far outdoes the discomfort of the mostly unpaved 'highway'.

Upon leaving Kangding in the early hours of the morning, the bus weaves its way up and over the Guoda Mountain pass as it heads into the valleys beyond. Looking back on a clear morning, the sun rises behind the mountain and rays of light spear over the peak. Leaving the jagged, snow-capped peaks behind, the route emerges into a narrow, verdant valley, gauged out of the towering mountain slopes by a fierce melt-water river that surges through. For 150km the road snakes its way through the valley, where huge, mansion-like houses belie their more humble agricultural roots, fields of wheat, barley and sun-flowers creating a patchwork of colour. Free-roaming livestock clatter up and down the road, unperturbed by the infrequent passing of traffic, and children come out to wave.

After several hours, the road suddenly emerges from the narrow valley into what is the start of the Tibetan plateau, where bright green mountain mead-ows gently roll away into the seemingly never-ending distance. Sedentary

farms give way to sparse nomadic tent settlements and the large stone stupas seen throughout the valleys become sporadic prayer flags, ragged and faded from the whipping wind and intense sunlight that characterises the region.

The bus slowly bounces along the road, gradually climbing the gargantuan peaks and passes, heading further and further into the wilderness of the high Tibetan plateau. At over 4000m above sea level, it is not only the intense beauty of the region that leaves visitors breathless, and light-headedness is a normal consequence of traversing the highway. As the road leads towards the remote town of Litang, the topography suddenly changes. As the bus sweeps around the final pass, vast grasslands stretch out in front, the town snuggled away in the shelter of the mountains that border the sprawling plateau.

Litang marks the end of the first phase of the highway and travel after this point becomes considerably harder. The rudimentary roads of the last 300km seem like a godsend compared with the route that lies ahead. From Litang the highway sprawls for another 1,486km until reaching Tibet's capital of Lhasa (although crossing the China Tibet border at Chubalong is not as easy as in other places and not recommended). Finding transport to Batang, the next town along at 165km away and 36km from the border, is relatively easy, but the road is hard-going and long but, as always, nature puts on a pretty good show to make sure you don't regret a single minute of the trip.

Litang

理塘

*L*ocated in the far reaches of the Sichuan Province, in what was once the ancient Tibetan lands of Kham, Litang is about as high and remote as towns get. As the South Sichuan-Tibet Highway rounds the final bend in its arduous yet breathtaking journey from Kangding, the Litang grasslands stretch out in front, the town nestled into the crook of the mountain below.

Litang has a population of 50,000, comprised almost wholly of Tibetans. Walking around the vibrant, busy little town provides the opportunity for some of the most fascinating people-watching opportunities in the province. Nomadic Tibetan cowboys have long since exchanged their trusty steeds for fast, shiny motorbikes and roar up and down the main street, coloured ribbons flapping from the handlebars, before heading off into the heart of the grasslands where their vast yak herds await them. Red gowned monks, members of the famous Ganden Thubchen Choerkhorling Monastery that looms high above the town, wander the streets, mobile phones in hand. Yak, pigs and packs of dogs idle down the roads oblivious to the noise and hustle and bustle around them. Old men sit on doorsteps playing cards, their concentration never flickering as small children shout 'hello' to their foreign visitors before running away giggling. Shops line the pavements, brightly coloured jewellery and handicrafts hanging from every spare inch and Chinese restaurants pump out spicy aromas.

Concerns

Litang sits at a whopping 4017m above sea level and altitude sickness is an unfortunate but undeniable factor of travel in this region. Be sure to give yourself time to acclimatise before doing any strenuous activity (see p106). Litang's climate is harsh and warm clothing is a must. Strong winds whip across the grasslands and snow and hail storms are frequent. Temperatures rarely exceed 15°C and can reach as low as -10°C during the night when the warmth of the sun disappears. Sunglasses and sunscreen are highly recommended as the sun is strong and vicious, unhindered by the lack of clouds.

Rival groups of young Tibetans occasionally get physical, but this is almost never directed towards foreign visitors and is generally a battle of turf. In any case, keep an eye on your belongings and take normal precautionary measures when travelling to remote areas.

Discover Litang

Horse Festival

Litang's horse festival is by far its most famous event and every year thousands of Tibetans (as well as Chinese and foreign visitors) come to take part in the festivities and celebrations. The festival's main draw is the horse events, where nomads come to strut their stuff, race along the dusty grasslands and demonstrate stunts to the throngs of raucous, appreciative spectators. Dressed in their vibrantly coloured finery, riders and horses compete for reputation over prizes. It is at the festival where young women come in search of husbands and successful riders often receive significant attention. Girls demonstrate their wealth and standing by adorning themselves with enormous amounts of expensive, colourful jewellery, often compiled from all members of the family.

A vast, sprawling tent city is erected just outside of town and is the temporary home of an important and prosperous trade fair. Anything and everything is brought here to be sold, bought or exchanged and it is possible to spend hours ambling through the noisy, packed tents taking in all the sights and sounds of Litang's most famous and highly anticipated event.

Ganden Thubchen Choekhorling Monastery

The monastery has an unmistakable presence as it sits regally on the hill rising to the north of the town. The vast complex was originally built in 1580 but has since been heavily reconstructed. The monastery holds great importance in Tibetan Buddhism having been the birthplace of several important Buddhists. The hall of fame includes the 7th and 10th Dalai Lamas, the 7th Gyamuyung Lama, the 7th, 8th and 9th Pabalha living Buddhas of the Chamdo Monastery and the 1st, 2nd and 3rd Xianggen living Buddhas.

The monastery is a beautiful example of a thriving, serene house of worship and the extremely amenable lamas welcome visitors with open arms to experience prayer sessions and tour the complex. Unlike many other Buddhist temples and monasteries, photos are permit-

ted (if you don't use the flash) and many monks enjoy posing for photos (in exchange for seeing the digital images afterwards). Apart from the multitude of halls, temples and shrines which are certainly worth looking at, be sure not to miss paying a visit to the kitchen (which is located to the right of the main hall) as it is provides a fascinating insight into day-to-day monastic life and an contrastive image to that of the ritualistic halls.

Maoya Prairie

About two hours by car from Litang is the Maoya Prarie. This vast, wild land is home to small clans of nomadic herdsmen who tend their yak herds, following their migrations through the seasons. The herds can range from tens of animals to groups over 200 strong, an impressive sight to behold as they stomp across the grasslands and weaving rivers.

There are plenty of drivers in Litang to take you out to see the yak herds. Whilst there are closer nomadic settlements, the bigger herds wander the lands further afield and the extra journey deposits visitors into the heart of a remote wilderness, an unparalleled experience in a country with such a staggering population. Black yak skin tents are home to bareback riding cowboys and their families, for whom life on the move is an ancestral privilege.

Sky Burial

Whispers of sky burial rituals seem to reach visitors long before they arrive in Litang, Dege (see p294) or Baotang and a morbid fascination seems inevitable. While attending a sky burial is, in most places, not allowed by outsiders, locals in Litang seem to be more than content for visitors to respectfully witness the ritual. Ask around locally to find out if any are scheduled during your stay. Mr. Zhang's restaurant is a good start, as Mr Zhang speaks rather good, self-taught English and serves some simple Western dishes. He is a fountain of enthusiastic knowledge and can answer any questions thrown at him. You will find his small restaurant to the right of Crane's Hotel and Hostel.

Sky burials are a Tibetan Buddhist form of body disposal that involves the cutting up of the human corpse which is then placed high on mountain tops and left to the elements, or more often, offered to vultures and other birds of prey. While in many societies this appears to be an unnecessary and rather gruesome ritual, Buddhism beliefs see the body merely as a vessel, one that is emptied and no longer needed after death and the disintegration of the soul. Known in Tibetan as *jhator* or 'giving alms to the birds', sky burials are seen as an act of generosity where the deceased and their relatives offer food to other living creatures. Vultures too are perceived differently to the way they are seen in other cultures and are considered to live by the fundamental ethics of Buddhism: not to kill a living being and to accept what one receives.

Horse Riding

A lovely day's horse trekking can be started from 12km out of town and takes visitors and their steeds to the small, remote Taka Monastery and Big Stupa. Local guides offer their services at reasonable prices and often speak English as well as Tibetan and Chinese. Ask at any hotel reception for recommendations and contacts.

Genie Mountain

The vast Genie Mountain rises proudly above the skyline of jagged peaks, its summit snow-capped year-round. A few kilometres out of town a dusty road crosses the grasslands and disappears into the distance, heading towards the holy mountain, long since a destination for throngs of devout worshippers. It is possible to hire drivers to get out into the mountain range and visit the lower slopes of Genie Mountain where Buddhists fervently pray, but trekking is extremely difficult due to the harsh climate, unforgiving terrain and intense altitude.

Daocheng and Yading Nature Reserve 稻城亚丁自然保护区
🕐 *Open from April – late October;* 💴 *8RMB*

The Yading Nature Reserve, located in southern Daocheng County, is often dubbed 'the last Shangri La' due to its extreme beauty. This truly untouched area of the country is vast. At the very least two days are needed to explore the park, and camping or taking advantage of the tent-hotels are the only forms of accommodation within the park boundaries. Small, simple restaurants are available however, so there is no need to take your own food. Horses can be hired for between 30-80RMB per day and are the preferred way of getting around. This sprawling expanse of wild terrain that has yet to see the influxes of visitors that have ravaged other beauty spots

(its sheer inaccessibility and remoteness playing the biggest part in this) and is home to three sacred mountains; Xinnairi (6032m), Yangmaiyong (5958m) and Chanadorje (5958m). Lakes, rivers, plateaus, glacial valleys, mountain meadows and imposing snow-capped peaks combine to form one of the country's most untamed and breathtaking landscapes.

Buses leave from Litang to Daocheng (4 hours) and from there cars can be hired to take you to the park entrance (2 hours). Be sure to arrange a car to pick you up after your visit as there is little or no transport outside the park. Severe weather conditions mean the reserve is only staffed between April and late October and surrounding roads are closed at other times of the year. Weather can be cold year round, especially at night, so come prepared.

Accommodation

Finding somewhere to stay in Litang is easy unless you happen to have arrived during the horse festival. At this time prices soar and rooms are fully booked weeks ahead.

Crash out or Splash out

Crane's Hotel and Hostel 仙鹤宾馆 *Tel: 0836-5321798; located 100m up from the bus station on the opposite side of the street; hotel price: low season/horse festival 80RMB/350RMB dbl; 150RMB/500RMB deluxe suite; hostel price: 20RMB dorm.* Accommodating any pocket Crane's tends to be most foreigners' first choice. Staff speak good English and can help find drivers or guides for the area. Hotel rooms are clean but basic and not particularly well heated. Dorms also come with TV, heated blanket and hot water.

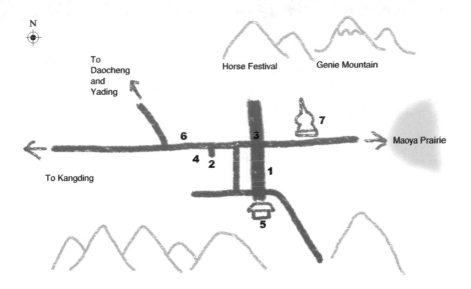

N

To Daocheng and Yading

Horse Festival   Genie Mountain

6   3   7

4 2

To Kangding   1   Maoya Prairie

5

1. Internet
2. Crane's hotel
3. Crane Square
4. Mr. Zheng's restaurant

5. Ganden Thobchen Choekhorling Monastery
6. Bus station
7. Big stupa

Hailuogou National Glacier Forest Park

Hailuogou National Glacier Forest Park
海螺沟国家森林公园

📞 Tel: 836- 3266550; @ www.hailuogou.com; last bus leaves the base at 18.00; ¥ 70RMB entrance, 70RMB bus

*D*escending from the great slopes of the majestic Gongga Mountain, glaciers fill the Hailuogou valley, carving their own path through the dense, virgin forests.

The Hailuogou Valley, which translates as 'Conch Gully', is located on the eastern side of the great Gongga Mountain and rises 6000m up the 7556m high giant. Due to this great altitude, the valley has seven different climatic zones which are each conducive to the growth of different species of vegetation and animals. In winter, snow blankets the ground and temperatures drop to well below zero, the landscape taking on a quiet, icy beauty as it awaits the spring melt. Summer temperatures average 25°C and plants and animals come alive, covering the valley in splashes of colour.

A 30km road winds up the valley stopping at base number 1, 2 and 3 where hotels and hot springs are based. Views of the Gongga Mountain on a clear day are spectacular from base No 3, especially at sunrise when the snow-capped peaks take on a golden hue. Buses link the bases and take approximately 1 hour to reach base No 3 and the cable car.

Discover Hailuogou

Grand Glacier Cascade

The largest glacier in the Hailuogou Valley, the Grand Glacier Cascade is renowned as being one of Asia's lowest glaciers, the tip of its 6km long tongue stretching as far down the valley to a mere 2,850m above sea level. The glaciers in this region, at 16 million years old, are classified as modern and are of a type found generally at low latitudes or altitudes. The viewing area for the Grand Glacier Cascade (also referred to as glacier No 1) is several kilometres away as regular and violent avalanches crash down the valley causing blue sparks of electricity, a splendid demonstration of Mother Nature's power. Access to the glacier is by cable car (160RMB roundtrip) which starts a few kilometres above base No 3 or by a very pleasant walk through the thick blanket of forest that swirls around the base of the glacier (1 hour). The walk provides stunning views of the lower glaciers as well as waterfalls, pools and the abundance of plant species that thrive here. It is possible to take a half hour guided tour on the lower fringes of the glacier where you can visit the ice tunnel and look down into some ominous crevasses (the tour is included in the entry ticket). Bigger hotels rent snow boots and overcoats as it can get extremely cold up on the glacier. If you don't rent boots be sure to wear appropriate footwear as the ice can be slippery and hazardous.

Hot sPrings

Strong tectonic movement in the Gongga Mountain region has resulted in the emergence of countless hot spring pools dotted all over the Hailuogou Valley. The most popular and convenient are those located within the Gongga Magic Spring Hotel at base No 2 (65RMB/free to hotel guests). A series of cascading, circular plunge pools and larger swimming pools range in temperature up to a blistering 50°C. Steam rises off the pools into the cooler mountain air and in winter the ground is blanketed by snow and ice. Dressing rooms are located a short distance away for those icy days when temperatures rest somewhere below zero and it is a frosty walk in swimwear to the warmth of the pools. Hot springs can also be found at base No 1.

Shuihaizi Lake

Heading up from the hot springs an ice lake sits amidst an untouched forest where Chinese yew, Katsura trees, Kangding Magnolia and big-leafed azalea fill the air with their strong scents. 400 species of animals live in this forest, in-

cluding 28 that are considered endangered. The quiet surroundings of this less-visited section of the park provide the best opportunities for spotting blue sheep, cheeky macaque monkeys and, very occasionally, red or giant pandas.

Accommodation

Plenty of small cheaper hostels and hotels can be found in Moxi at the base of the valley, while the pricier establishments can be found within the park. Moxi also has several guesthouses which offer cheap accommodation. Hotels and hostels tend to suffer serious damp problems and hot water is limited even in the more expensive ones.

Crash out

Ask around for guesthouses which range between 20 – 100RMB per night. They range considerably in quality so it's best to look at a few before making a choice.

Splash out

Gongga Magic Spring Hotel 海螺沟 贡嘎温泉宾馆 *Tel: 836- 3266170; price 420RMB standard room/560RMB deluxe cabin* Located at base No 2 this 4*hotel is undoubtedly the classiest in the area and it comes with the added luxury of the hot springs. If you can run to a deluxe cabin, they come with their own private outdoor pool.

On the Road

Buses leave from Chengdu Xinnanmen Bus Station (100RMB/5-6 hours) direct to the national park entrance in Moxi. The once daily return bus to Chengdu leaves at 6am. If you miss this bus you can hire a private car to Gan'gudi (20RMB) where regular Chengdu-bound buses

stop. Buses to Luding 52km away leave from Chengdu's Chadianzi Bus Station where you can visit the Luding Bridge (see p324) and then hop on a minibus to Moxi (25RMB/2 hours). There are no direct buses from Kangding but blue taxis will take you to Luding (25RMB/2 hours) where you can change to a Moxi-bound minibus.

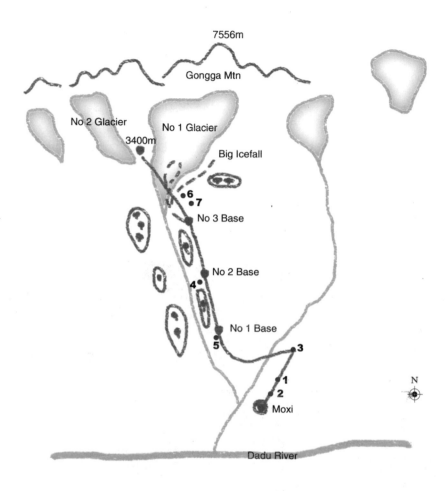

7556m

Gongga Mtn

No 2 Glacier

No 1 Glacier

3400m

Big Icefall

● 6
● 7

No 3 Base

No 2 Base

4 ●

No 1 Base

5

3

1

2

Moxi

N

Dadu River

1. Ticket office
2. Hotel booking offices
3. Bus Station
4. Gongga Mogio Spring Hotel
5. Hot springs

6. Cable car
7. Scenic walk
Virgin Forests
River / glacier

Around Hailuogou

Luding Bridge 泸定桥

¥ 10RMB

"Victory was life, defeat was certain death" - Red Army General Peng Dehuai.

*T*he fierce and heroic battle that took place at Luding is one that has gone down in Chinese history books as marking a significant advancement of the Chinese Red Army's Long March in 1934-35. Upon Mao Zedong's orders that the bridge at Luding was to be taken by force, soldiers of the 4th Regiment marched a gruesome and exhausting 120km in 24 hours under General Lin Bao's leadership.

In the early hours of 29th May, 1935, with only a third of the regiment having survived the arduous march, soldiers arrived in Luding to find the town occupied by troops from the Kuomintang and the planks having been removed from the bridge.

Undeterred, 22 Red Army soldiers crawled across the 300 year old bridge, clinging to raw chains under intense machine gun fire from forces on the other side of the ferocious Dadu River. While several were injured, they surged ahead launching a torrent of grenades into the heart of their enemy until finally taking control of the bridge. On June 2, 1935 the entire Red Army completed its crossing of Luding Bridge. Today, 22 pillars stand in the Luding Bridge memorial museum in honour of the brave men who many consider to have been vital in the ultimate success of the Red Army. While four of the pillars are engraved with the names of those who battled so hard, 18 remain blank, their names forever unknown.

South Sichuan Bamboo Sea

South Sichuan Bamboo Sea 蜀南竹海风景区
Tel: 0831-4980888; @ *www.bamboosea.net; open; price*

*T*he South Sichuan Bamboo Sea is most aptly named. Stretching away into the horizon, the waves of peaks and valleys are covered by a thick, mint-coloured bamboo blanket. Mist settles in the troughs, hanging above the trees and lakes, waterfalls and cliffs, creating an aura of tranquillity.

The South Sichuan Bamboo Sea is as yet relatively undiscovered by the vast tour groups that frequent so many of China's other top destinations, and finding peace and quiet is easy. Privately hired minibuses (100RMB/day/6people) tootle along the leafy roads that wind through the enormous park taking visitors to the most beautiful landscapes this region has to offer. 400 different species of bamboo thrive here forming a densely woven canopy under which other plants and animals take refuge and caves, temples, springs and mirror-like lakes find their nook. Keep your eyes open for Bamboo monkeys and several different species of frogs which can be heard chattering and croaking as you walk through the park's paths. 6000 people live within the far reaches of the park and their gentle influence adds a touch of civilisation to the exuberance of nature. Handmade bamboo crafts are lovely keepsakes and sold at extremely reasonable prices.

Discover the South Sichuan Bamboo Sea

Emerald Long Corridor

The red soils that characterise the park's geology are here exaggerated in their contrast to the tunnel of bamboo leaves that link overhead, providing a lovely walk.

Cloud Viewing Pavilion

For the best view of the vast expanse of forest and hills that stretch for 120km before you, the Cloud Viewing Pavilion is the place to go. Sunset is the best time to go if the weather is clear and visibility is good.

Forget–Your–Worries Valley

As the name suggests, this is one of the most tranquil and relaxing walks in the park. The small winding paths that weave through the towering, multi-coloured bamboo stems follow the course of a lovely little stream that trickles over rocks and waterfalls.

Rainbow Waterfall

This large series of cascades roars down the valley, pushing aside vegetation as it carves its course in its hurried path downhill. The 10m wide falls form a total height of 81m, an impressive and worthwhile sight to behold.

A Lake in a Sea

This large lake is most popular for its boating opportunities, allowing visitors to get off the road and out into the heart of the park. Long, flat-bottomed bamboo rafts cause much entertainment as visitors attempt to navigate them around the still waters of the lake.

Buddhism

Ancient shrines, statues of Buddha, cultural relics and rock caves are dotted all over the park, evidence of a lasting and active site of Buddhist worship. A walk down to the Heavenly Treasure Cave in the GuaBang Rock Caves is one of the highlights, where temples

have been intricately carved from the rose-coloured cliff face and Buddhist symbology complements the natural surroundings. Be sure not to miss the Immortal Residence Cave, where a vast Buddha sleeps peacefully opposite a sweeping view of the valleys below.

Accommodation

The Bamboo Sea is located 2 hours drive from the town of Yibin so makes for an easy day trip. Most people stay in Yibin which has a vast array of hotels on offer and is a pleasant, if not fascinating place to spend a couple of nights. There are however places to stay closer to the park if you plan to spend a couple of days there.

Crash out
Zhuhai Binguan竹海宾馆
Tel: 0831-4980000; 30-70RMB offers cheap rooms within the boundary of the park entrance. It's simple but clean and provides for some extremely peaceful and quiet surroundings.

Splash out
Shunan Binguan 蜀南宾馆
Tel: 0831-4980555; 300RMB/double. Offers the best accommodation and is located close to the west gate. Comfortable, well equipped rooms, friendly service and a large restaurant complete the package.

On the Road

The park is located in Shunan Zhuhai, 330km from Chengdu and buses leave twice a day from Xinnanmen Bus Station (09.20 and 15.30/95RMB/4 hours). Alternatively, buses from Yibin leave regularly. To reach other sights in the region head back to Yibin. Buses to Zigong or Chengdu leave from Beimen Bus Station 北门 汽车站.

Around the South Sichuan Bamboo Sea

Zigong Dinosaur Museum 自贡恐龙博物馆
Tel: 86-813-5801235/5802095; www.zdm.cn; open 08. 00-17.30; price 40RMB

Important dinosaur discoveries in the 1980s led to the town of Zigong becoming nationally and internationally renowned and a huge museum dedicated to all things dinosaur has become its top tourist attraction. It became the first and only dinosaur-dedicated museum in all Asia and a dinosaur was even named after the township, Dashanpusaurus. While the museum itself is very good and highly informative, the models outside are certainly designed for younger children.

Xingwen Karst Geological Park and the Hanging Coffins of the Bo People 兴文国家地质公园及悬棺

Black wooden coffins hanging precariously from a vertical cliff are all that remain of a 3000 year old mysterious ethnic minority known as the Bo People. Long since having died out, the coffins are all that remain of the people that have left archaeologists and ethnographers baffled. The practice of hanging coffins separated the Bo people from other minorities and the practice died out 400 years ago, at the same time as the Bo people mysteriously disappeared. The oldest coffins in this region date to the Song Dynasty (1000 years ago) although similar ones found in Yunnan's Three Gorges area date back 2,500 years to the Spring and Autumn Period.

The park itself is a fascinating and strangely beautiful place to spend a day. Unique limestone formations, gorges, waterfalls, lakes, karst caves and an array of unusual plant species add to the mystery and fascination created by the Bo people who lived in the region for centuries.

The geological park is located in Yibin's Gongxian County approximately 2 hours south of the Bamboo Sea. Local buses from Yibin will take you out there or private cars can be hired from the Bamboo Sea.

Three Kingdoms Tour

$\mathcal{T}$he Three Kingdoms period (220-280) was a crucial part of Chinese history (see p22) and Sichuan formed the backdrop for many of the historical events, as well as being the political, cultural and military centre of the Shu state at the time. Today, a fascinating tour of these historical and cultural sites provides an insight into a 2,000 year old heritage that has exerted considerable influence over China and its people. A tour of the major sites takes visitors on a circular route beginning and ending in Chengdu and takes at least three days.

Chengdu

Chengdu acted as capital of state of Shu during the Three Kingdoms period and marks the first stop along the tour.

Marquis Wu's Shrine (Wuhou Temple 武侯祠)

The shrine was built to commemorate the Shu state's prime minister Zhuge Liang's prowess as a politician, ideologist and strategist (see p84). He has become the embodiment of wisdom and courage and countless legends relating to him have been handed down through the generations.

Deyang

德阳

*D*uring the Three Kingdoms period Deyang was under the jurisdiction of the state of Shu and a violent battle launched by Liu Bei was waged here. The ancient archaeological site of Sanxingdui (see p194) is located nearby and is a must-see in order to make some sense of the complex history of this time.

Pang Tong's Shrine and Tomb 庞统祠

The shrine, also known as Marquis Jing's Shrine, was dedicated to the man who became Liu Bei's military advisor. Upon following Liu Bei into Sichuan, Pang Tong made history for his capture of generals Yang Huai and Gao Pei and his leading of troops towards Chengdu. He was struck by an arrow in a fierce battle and it is popular belief that he died on the spot where his tomb stands today.

Two Loyal Generals' Shrine 双忠祠

The shrine was erected to commemorate the revered generals Zhuge Zhan and his son Zhuge Shang. They are best remembered for sacrificing their lives in the defence of Sichuan in a mighty battle at Mianyang Pass against the Cao Wei general Deng Ai.

Other Places to Visit

Guanghan Sanxingdui Museum 广汉三星堆博物馆
Deyang Confucian Temple 德阳文庙
Yinghua Mountain Scenic Area

On the Road

Trains leave Chengdu's North Railway Station to Deyang daily (11RMB/1 hour).

Mianyang

绵阳

Mianyang served as a crucial strategic thoroughfare on the Sichuan Road during the Three Kingdoms period. It was a major strongpoint along Liu Bei's march towards Sichuan and was the strategic headquarters in Jiang Wan's battle against troops from the state of Wei.

Jiang Wan's Tomb 蒋琬墓

Jiang Wan was a high-ranking official of the state of Shu and after Zhuge Liang's death he played an important role in the leadership of the state. Upon his death he was buried on the Western Hill in Mianyang.

Fule Mountain and Hall 富乐山

The Fule Mountain public park marks the spot where Liu Zhang and Liu Bei met upon Liu Bei's arrival in the province. He entered Sichuan under the intention of helping Liu Zhang in his battle against Cao Cao. The name Fule, meaning 'rich and happy' derives from a famous statement made by Liu Bei whilst admiring the lands in front of him 'What a rich land! I am so happy to see it today.'

On display are a telling selection of clay sculptures depicting the great meeting, as well as statues of five famous generals of the state of Shu: Guan Yu, Zhang Fei, Ma Chao, Huang Zhong and Zhao Yun.

Other Places to Visit

Ancient Qinglian Town – hometown of Li Bai. 李白故里

On the Road

There are daily shuttle buses which leave from Chengdu's Zhaojue Temple Bus Terminal to Mianyang and its surrounding attrations.

Guangyuan

广元

*T*here are over 140 historical sites scattered in the vicinity of the area and it is both a picturesque and interesting place to visit. The stunning landscape makes a wonderful backdrop for the historic sites and is a beautiful place to spend a few days.

Jianmen Pass 剑门关

The 72 jagged peaks that form the Jianmen Pass created a natural, impassable barrier along the ancient Sichuan Road, and ruins of Zhuge Liang's Pass are still evident. Shu state general Jiang Wei once used the powerful natural barrier to hold off the 100,000-strong Wei army troops that were attempting to cross it.

Cuiyun Corridor 翠云廊

8,000 vast, ancient cypress trees line the sides of the 100km long old post road, awarding it the nickname 'Imperial Cypress Avenue'. Legend has it the trees were planted by Zhang Fei's soldiers during the Three Kingdoms period.

Other Places to Visit

Thousand-Buddha precipice 千佛崖
Bright Moon Gorge 明月峡

On the Road

There are regular buses leaving Chengdu's Zhaojue Temple Bus Station daily.

Langzhong

阆中

*T*he town is most well known for the famous general Zhang Fei. During the Three Kingdoms period, he is said to have stationed himself in Langzhong for seven years.

Marquis Huan's Shrine (Zhang Fei's Shrine) 桓侯祠

Zhang Fei was a sworn ally of Liu Bei and ranked second of five of the Shu state's most important officials. He was killed by his aides in 221 and buried here. Following his death, Liu Bei's son, Liu Chan, honoured him with the name Marquis Huan.

Other Places to Visit

Old City of Langzhong 阆中古城
Baba Temple 巴巴寺

On the Road

Buses to Langzhong leave regularly from Chengdu's Shiling Bus Station.

Nanchong

南充

Nanchong is famed as being the place where Chen Shou wrote the masterpiece *History of the Three Kingdoms*. Because of this, this ancient city has been dubbed 'the birthplace of the Three-Kingdom culture'.

Wanjuan Tower in Western Hill 西山万卷楼

According to popular belief, this is the exact spot where Chen Shou wrote his world-famous novel. Today a 5m high statue of him and copious amounts of cultural relics relating to his famous work are on display.

Other Places to Visit

Western Hill Scenic Area
Giant Buddha in the Garden of Steles

On the Road

Daily buses leave Chengdu's Zhaojue Temple Bus Station.

Three-Kingdom's Tour

Ancient Plank Roads 古栈道
Bright Moon Gorge 明月峡

Thousand-Buddha Precipice 千佛崖
Huangze Temple 皇泽寺

Guangyuan 广元

44

昭化古城
Old Zhaohua City

Sword Pavilion 剑阁

14

剑门关 Jianmen Pass
翠云廊 Cuiyun Corridor

5

293(成广高速)
293(Chengdu-Guangyuan Expressway)

108

40

Hometown of Li Bai 李白故里

Marquis Huan's Shrine 桓侯祠
Old City Area 古城区

57

富乐山 Fule Mountain
蒋琬墓 Jiang Wan's Tomb

阆中
Langzhong

32

Pang Tong's Shrine
庞统祠

双忠祠
Two Loyal
Generals's
Shrine

60

文庙 Confucian Temple

德阳
Deyang

64

三星堆
Sanxingdui

21

广汉 Guanghan

42

万卷楼 Wanjuan Tower
西山 Western Hill

41

成都 Chengdu

南充 Nanchong

武侯祠
Marquis Wu's Shrine

200(成南高速)
200(Chengdu-Nanchong Expressway)

THE GUIDE

Language Guide

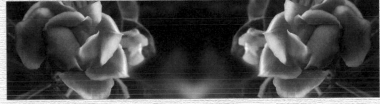

Handy Phrases

China in general, and Sichuan in particular, can be a very difficult place to get around if no-one in your party speaks Mandarin. Sichuan also has a second linguistic trap- many parts of Western Sichuan still speak Tibetan as the primary language. Although English is taught in schools, finding someone conversationally fluent can be quite difficult. If you have an immediate emergency, contacting the English teacher of the local middle school can help- they may not speak the language fluently, but they can certainly read and write it to a high standard.

Getting by day-to-day can be a trying experience, so below we have endeavoured to include some basic phrases in Mandarin and Tibetan to help you get by.

Basics

Hello
Ni hao 你好
khyed bde mo

Goodbye
Zai Jian 再见
bde mo

My name is
Wo de mingze shi/Wo jiao
我的名字是 / 我叫
ngvi ming la

Thanks
Xie Xie 谢谢
thugs rje che

Yes
Shi 是
red

No
Bu 不
ma red

You're welcome
Bu ke qi 不客气
snng dg med

Excuse me
Dui bu qi 对不起
Thugs rgy ma bzhengs
dgongs pa ma tshom

Me
Wo 我
nga

He
ta 他
khong

Us
Women 我们
nga tsho

She
ta 她
kho mo

You
Ni 你
khged

Them
Tamen 他们 / 她们
kho tsho

Do you speak English?
Ni hui bu hui shuo yingyu?
你会不会说英语?
Khyed kyis dbyin skd bshde shes

I know/Don't know
Wo zhidao/bu zhidao
我知道 / 不知道
Ngs shes/mi shes

Is there an English translator here?
You meiyou yingyu fanyi?
有没有英语翻译?
Dbyin ji skd bsgyur ba e yod

I'm sorry, I don't speak Chinese.
Bu hao yisi, wo bu hui shuo hanyu.
不好意思，我不会说汉语
Dgongs pa ma tshom,noys dbyin skd rggs mi shes

How do you say —— in Mandarin?
zhongwen zenme shuo?
中文怎么说?
Rgy skd la ga vdr bshd dgos

I'm lost!
Wo milu le!
我迷路了
ngs lm nor song

Where is the toilet?
Cesuo zai nar?
厕所在哪?
Spyod khng gng na yod

Numbers

1	Yi, Yao	一	gcig
2	Er, Liang	二 / 两	gnyis
3	San	三	gsum
4	Si	四	bzhi
5	Wu	五	lng
6	Liu	六	drug
7	Qi	七	bdun
8	Ba	八	brgyd
9	Jiu	九	dgu
10	Shi	十	bcu
100	Yi Bai	一百	brgya
200	Liang Bai	两百	nyis brgya
300	San Bai	三百	sum brgya
400	Si Bai	四百	bzhi brgya
500	Wu Bai	五百	lng brgya
1,000	Yi Qian	一千	stong gcig
10,000	Yi Wang	一万	khri gcig

Days of the Week

Monday	Xingqiyi	星期一	gzv zla ba
Tuesday	Xingqier	星期二	gzv mig dmr
Wednesday	Xingqisan	星期三	gzv lhg pa
Thursday	Xingqisi	星期四	gzv phur bu
Friday	Xingqiwu	星期五	gzv pa sngs
Saturday	Xingqiliu	星期六	gzv spen pa
Sunday	Xingqiri	星期日	gzv nyi ma
Today	Jintian	今天	de ring
Tomorrow	Mingtian	明天	sng nging
Yesterday	Zuotian	昨天	kha sng

Times of Day

Morning	Zaoshang/Shangwu	早上／上午	zhogs pa /sng dro
Noon	Zhongwu	中午	nyin gung
Afternoon	Xiawu	下午	phyi dro
Evening	Wanshang	晚上	dgung mo

Directions

Straight ahead
Yizhi zou
一直走
thd kr song

Turn left
Zuo zhuan
左转
gyong la vkhor

Turn right
You zhuan
右转
gys la vkhor

Opposite
Duimianr
对面
ng thug

Behind
Houbianr
后边
rgbs phyogs

Near the market
Shichang fujin
市场附近
Tshong rvi nige vkhor

Near the bridge
Qiao fujin
桥附近
zm gyi nye vkhor

At the traffic lights
Zai honglvdeng
在红绿灯
glog dmr ljng

At the next corner
Zai xia yige guaijiao
在下一个拐角
vkhogs sne rjs ma

Stop here
Ting xialai
停下来
mtshms zhogs

Getting Around

Where is the bus/train station?
Qichezhan/huochezhan zai nali?
汽车站 / 火车站在哪里?
Rlngs vkhor sa tshigs sa tshigs gng na yod

I need a taxi
Wo yao dache
我要打车
ngs mo tr gla dgs me vkhor

What time is the bus to Kangding?
Qichequ Kangding shi shenme shihou?
汽车去康定是什么时候?
Rlngs vkhor dr rts md o la ga dus gtong rgyu red

Do you know a good (cheap) hotel?
Ni zhidao bu zhidao yige haode (pianyide) binguan?
你知不知道一个好的（便宜的）宾馆?
khyed kyis mgron khng yg pa yod sa e shes

Can you recommend a good restaurant?
Ni neng buneng tuijian yige fanguan?
你能不能推荐一个饭馆?
khyed kyis za knng zhig ngo sprod byed e thub

We'd like to hire a car/minivan/bike
Women yao zu yiliang qiche/mianbaoche/zixingche
我们要租一辆汽车 / 面包车 / 自行车
Nga tshos rlngs vkhor gcig gla dgos/ rkng vkhor

Booking a Hotel

I'd like to make a reservation...
Wo xiang ding yige fangjian...
我想订一个房间
ngs khng pa gcig gla rgyn yin

...for one/two/three/four/five nights
...yi/er/san/si/wu tian
一／二／三／四／五天
nyin gcig/gnyis/gsum/ bzhi/ lnga

Do you have a single/double room?
Nimen you meiyou yige danrenjian/shuangrenjian?
你们有没有一个单人间／双人间?
khyod tshor mi goyis vdug svi khng paeyod

Does it have a bathroom/western toilet?
Fangjian you meiyou weishengjian/matong cesuo?
房间有没有卫生间／马桶厕所?
Khng pvi nng du spyod khngeyod

Can I see the room?
Neng bu neng kanyikan fangjian?
能不能看一看房间?
Khng pa la blt e chog

Going Shopping

What is this?
Zhe shi shenme?
这是什么?
vdi ci red

Too expensive!
Tai gui la!太贵了!
Gong che drgs

How much is it?
Duo shao qian?
多少钱
sgor ga tshod red

Can you make it cheaper?
Neng buneng pianyi dian?
能不能便宜点?
gong mr bcgs e chog

Eating Out

Waiter!
Fuwuyuan!
服务员!
zhbs zhu pa

Can I see the menu?
Wo neng kankan caidan ma?
我能看看菜单吗?
ngs zs rin la blta e chog

Do you have an English menu?
You meiyou yingwen caidan?
有没有英文菜单?
db yin yig gi ze tho e yod

I'll have that dish
Wo dian nage cai
我点那个菜
ngs za ma gng bshd dgos

Can you bring me some chopsticks/a spoon?
Gei wo lai yishuang kuaize/yige shaozi
给我一双筷子/一个勺子
ngala thur ma gcig sprd dng /khem bu

Do you have a knife and fork?

You meiyou daocha?

有没有刀叉?

Gri chba e yod

I'd like a beer/ ice tea/coffee

Wo xiang yao yiping pijiu/ yiping bing hongcha/yibei kafei

我想要一瓶啤酒 / 瓶冰红茶 / 杯咖啡

Nga la pi rga dm bu gcig dgos/jadmr/kha hphe

I'd like to order beef noodles

Wo lai yifen niurou mian

我来一份牛肉面

nga la thug pa dkr yol grig dgos

What is a famous Sichuan dish?

You shenme Sichuan tesecai?

有什么四川特色菜?

Si khron gi za ma gng var yod

I'm a vegetarian

wo shi shi su de.

我是食素的

ngs sha mi za

I don't eat meat/drink alcohol

Wo bu chi huncai/he jiu

我不吃荤菜 / 喝酒

ngs she zsa mi za /chng vthng

Can I have the bill?

Maidan

买单

rtsi rgyob

Useful Information

Emergency Contact Numbers

Ambulance: 120
Police: 110
Fire: 119

English Speaking hospital:
Global Doctor Clinic Tel: 028-85226058

Government complaints hotline:12345

Consulates in Chengdu:

United States Consulate General
Add: 4 Consulate Road, Chengdu, Sichuan
Tel:028-85583992/85589642
HP: http://chengdu.usembassy-china.org.cn/
名称：美国驻成都总领事馆
地址：四川省成都市领事馆路4号
电话：028-85583992/8558964200

German Consulate General
Add: Floor 6, Western Union Building,No.19 Section 4,
Renming Nan Road
Tel:028-66801996
名称：德国驻成都总领事馆
地址：四川省成都市人民南路4段19号Western联邦大厦6楼
电话：028-66801996

France Consulate General
Add: Floor 30,Time Square,2 Zongfu Road, Chengdu, Sichuan
Tel:028-66666060
名称：法国驻成都总领事馆
地址：四川省成都市总府路2号时代广场30层
电话：028-66666060口口

Korea Consulate General
Add: Floor 19, Tianfulvzhou Building, 2 Xia Nan Road,
Chengdu, Sichuan
Tel:028-86165800
名称：韩国驻成都总领事馆
地址：四川省成都市下南大街2号天府绿洲大厦19层
电话：028-86165800口口

Thailand Consulate General
Add: Floor 2, Office Building, Kempinski Hotel, 42 Section 4,
Renming Nan Road
Tel:028-85192266
名称：泰国驻成都总领事馆
地址：四川省成都市人民南路4段42号凯宾斯基饭店办公楼2楼
电话：028-85192266

Calling Internationally

Many hotel rooms offer International Direct Dial (IDD) service to call abroad. Simply enter 00 followed by the country code, area code and number you wish to contact. Hotel prices for IDD calls can be quite high however, so you are best advised to purchase an IP card which provides cheaper international calls. There are several IP card providers offering different packages, but in general China Telecom is considered the best all-round choice. IP cards can be bought from local kiosk stores and can only be used in the area in which they were purchased. IP cards bought in the Chengdu area can't be used in Beijing for example. Instructions on how to use the cards is written on the back in English as well as Chinese but the table below provides an easy reference on the what, why's and how's of using IP cards.

Company Name: China Telecom
Price(RMB)Service Quality/Access Region: 1.50/min
Hong Kong, Macau and Taiwan: 2.40/min
America and Canada: 3.60*/min
Other major countries: 4.60/min

Company Name: China Unicom
Price(RMB)Service Quality/Access Region: 1.50/min2.40/min
Hong Kong, Macau and Taiwan: 3.60/min
America and Canada: 3.60/min
Other major countries: 4.60/min

Company Name: China Netcom
Price(RMB)Service Quality/Access Region: 1.50/min
Hong Kong, Macau and Taiwan: 2.40/min
America and Canada: 3.20/min
Other major countries: 4.20/min

*Britain, France, Italy, Germany, New Zealand, Korea, Japan, Australia, Singapore, Malaysia, Thailand, Indonesia, Philippines** Britain, France, Germany, New Zealand, Japan, Australia, Singapore

Steps to call:

China Telecom IP Card: China Unicom IP Card
Dial 17900/17908: Dial 17910
1.Mandarin 2. English: 1. Mandarin 2. English
Card number.: Card number.
PIN #: PIN #
IDD#: IDD#

China Telecom IP Card: China Unicom IP Card
Dial 17900/17908: Dial 17930
1.Mandarin 2. English: 1. Mandarin 2. English 3. Cantonese
Card number.: Card number.
PIN #: PIN #
IDD#: IDD# 1# Balance Query
        2# Password Change
        3# Balance Transfer

Chengdu Chadianzi Bus Timetable
成都茶店子汽车时刻表

Terminus	Distance (km)	Price (Yuan)	Time
Wolong	140	20.50 RMB	11:40
Wolong	140	21.00 RMB	11:40
Wolong	140	22.50 RMB	11:40
Maoxian	194	27.00 RMB	7:00 8:10 9:20 10:30 11:40 12:50 14:00 15:10
Maoxian	194	27.50 RMB	7:00 8:10 9:20 10:30 11:40 12:50 14:00 15:10
Maoxian	194	29.50 RMB	7:00 8:10 9:20 10:30 11:40 12:50 14:00 15:10
Songpan	335	45.00 RMB	6:30 7:00 7:30
Songpan	335	45.50 RMB	6:30 7:00 7:30
Songpan	335	49.00 RMB	6:30 7:00 7:30
Danba	351	71.00 RMB	6:30
Danba	351	——	6:30

Terminus	Distance (km)	Price (Yuan)	Time
Danba	351	——	6:30
Siguniang Mountain	270	——	
Siguniang Mountain	270	66.00RMB	8:20
Jiuzhaigou	270	——	8:20
Jiuzhaigou	438	——	8:40
Jiuzhaigou	438	92.00RMB	8:40
Dujiangyan	49	——	From 6:30 every 5 or minute
Dujiangyan	49	16.00RMB	From 6:30 every 5 or minute
Dujiangyan	49	——	From 6:30 every 5 or minute
Dujiangyan	55	16.00RMB	From 6:30 every 5 or minute
Dujiangyan	55	——	From 6:30 every 5 or minute
Qingcheng Mountain	55	——	From 6:30 every 5 or minute

Terminus	Distance (km)	Price (Yuan)	Time
Qingcheng Mountain	71	——	
Qingcheng Mountain	71	21.00RMB	8:30 9:30 10:30 15:30
Leshan	144	——	8:30 9:30 10:30 15:30
Leshan	144	——	8:30 9:30 10:30 15:30
Leshan	144	29.50RMB	8:30 9:30 10:30 15:30
Leshan	169	——	14:30
Leshan	169	26.50RMB	14:30
Leshan	169	——	14:30
Emei	143	——	8:20 13:20
Emei	143	27.50RMB	8:20 13:20
Emei	143	31.00RMB	8:20 13:20

Bus Travel Times

	Chengdu	Emei Shan	Jiuzhaigou	Songpan	Wolong	Danba	Kangding	Ganzi	Dege	Litang	Hailuoguo	Yibin
Chengdu												
Emei Shan	2 hours											
Jiuzhaigou	10 hours	12 hours										
Songpan	7hours	9 hours	3 hours									
Wolong	4 hours	6 hours	7 hours	5 hours								
Danba	6 hours	10 hours	12 hours	7 hours	5 hours							
Kangding	4hours	7 hours	16 hours	14 hours	9 hours	4 hours						
Ganzi	20hours	19 hours	34 hours	26 hours	21 hours	8 hours	12 hours					
Dege	2-3days	31 hours	40 hours	38 hours	33 hours	20 hours	24 hours	12 hours				
Litang	12hours	15 hours	24 hours	22 hours	17 hours	Direct	8 hours	Direct	Direct			
Hailuoguo	7 hours	6 hours	17 hours	14 hours	13 hours	8 hours	4 hours	16 hours	4 hours	12 hours		
Yibin	4 hours	6 hours	14 hours	11 hours	8 hours	12 hours	8 hours	24 hours	2-3 days	16 hours	8 hours	

Legend: Direct

Hours based on combined bus travel excluding transfer times or over-night stops.

Travel Information

AIR

Sichuan Airlines
Sichuan Airlines Co., Ltd
24H Line:028-88888888
Service Line:028-85393777
Fax:028-85393888
HP:www.scal.com.cn
Email:passenger@scal.com.cn

Air China
Service Line:+86) 4008 100 999
Tel:+86) 10 64595912
Fax:+86) 10 64569155
HP:www.airchina.com.cn
Email:complaint@mail.airchina.com.cn

Shuangliu International Airport
Flight Information: 028-85205333/555
Ticket hotline: 028-86668080
www.cdairport.com

Airport Shuttle Bus
Shuttle buses run to and from the city centre every 20 Minutes from 05.00 to the last plane of the day (30mins/10RMB). Buses to the airport leave from CAAC Air Ticket Office, Renmin Road.

TRAIN

Chengdu Railway Station
Renmin Road North
Information and tickets: 028-86433232
www.chengdustation.com - for internet ticket booking

BUS

Chadianzi Bus Station
Buses to: Dujiangyan, Mount Qingcheng, Aba and Garze Prefectures, west of the city.
Tel: 028-87506610

Xinnanmen Bus Station (Tourist Station)
Buses to: tourist sights all over the province and beyond
Tel: 028-85433609

Chengdu Bus Station
Buses to: Chongqing and areas east of Chengdu
Tel: 028-84711692

Zhaojue Bus Station
Buses to: Deyang, Mianyang, Jiangyou, Pingwu and areas north of Chengdu
Tel: 028-83504125

Suggested Itineraries

One Week

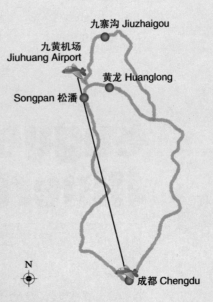

Begin your week in **Chengdu,** spending two days getting to know Sichuan's capital.

Fly to Jiuhuang Airport and spend two days visiting the spectacular **Jiuzhaigou National Park.**

Travel to **Huanglong National Park** allowing half a day to hike around the unique calcium pools.

Head south to the Hui Muslim town of **Songpan** and embark on a day's horse trip into the surrounding countryside.

Travel back to **Chengdu** on the morning bus and take in a **Sichuan Opera** performance in the evening to round off your trip.

Two Weeks

Songpan 松潘

丹巴 Danba

卧龙
Wolong

都江堰
Dujiangyan
Irrigation Project

青城山
Qingcheng Mountain

Chengdu 成都

Emeishan 峨眉山
Leshan 乐山

N

Follow the **1 week** itinerary to **Songpan.**

Take the bus to Dujiangyan and spend a day and a half visiting the **Dujiangyan Irrigation Project** and **Qingcheng Mountain.**

Take the bus to the **Wolong Panda Research Centre** and enjoy a day getting to know Sichuan's furriest residents.

Head over the precipitous Balang Mountain and follow the river all the way to **Danba.**

Spend a day in and around **Danba** visiting the Qiang villages and Suopo watchtowers.

Spend the day making your way to the holy **Emei Shan** where you will need two days to hike around the mountain, visit the countless temples and witness monkeys at their cheekiest.

Make the short the journey to the **Leshan Giant Buddha** where you can spend a few hours before heading back to Chengdu.

One Month

Days 1 - 3: Spend three days exploring and getting to know **Chengdu.** Be sure not to miss the Wenshu Temple, Jinsha ruins and Dufu's Cottage, some of the city's highlights.

Day 4: Hop on an early flight to Jiuhuang Airport and spend the afternoon hiking around the stunning calcium pools of **Huanglong** before heading on to Jiuzhaigou town.

Days 5 - 6: Spend two days exploring the **Jiuzhaigou Valley** with its breathtaking scenery, abundance of walking trails and rich cultural heritage.

Day 7: Head out to the traditional **Langzhai village** early in the morning, before catching a bus to Songpan.

Day 8: Spend the day visiting **Songpan**, walking the cobbled streets and taking in the feel of this ancient city. If time allows, a horse trek into the surrounding countryside is an unforgettable experience.

Day 9: Rise early and spend the day making your way to Wolong.

Day 10: Spend the day at the **Wolong Panda Research Centre** getting to know Sichuan's furriest residents.

Day 11: Head back to Chengdu early and then change to Kangding bound bus.

Day 12: Spend the day in **Kangding**, Sichuan's gateway to the west. Visit Racehorse Hill and soak up the eclectic mix of people, religions and architecture.

Day 13: Choose one of two routes; a) the **South Sichuan-Tibet Highway** or b) the **North Sichuan-Tibet Highway**. Take an early morning bus heading towards a) **Litang** (arriving in the afternoon) or b) **Dege** (a two day journey that will overnight you in **Ganzi, Manigange** and **Luhuo**).

Day 14: a) Spend the day in **Litang** visiting the famous Buddhist monastery and enjoying the rural Tibetan charm of this small town b) Continue onwards and upwards to Dege over the beautiful Himalayan foothills and over the precipitous Cho La Pass.

Day 15: a) Take a trip out to the Maoya Prairie and see the vast yak herds that live in the wild Tibetan hinterlands b) visit the Batong Scripture Lamasery or take a hike through some of the surrounding countryside.

Day 16: a) Take a guided horse trip out into the sweeping plains of the grasslands and if you're lucky, witness a traditional sky burial b) Make your way back to **Ganzi** and spend the afternoon visiting the massive Ganzi Temple .

Day 17: a) Head back towards Kangding taking a detour to **Tagong** and its shimmering gold temple and sprawling grasslands b) spend the day in Ganzi, relaxing and shopping.

Day 18: a) Enjoy a day hiking in the stunning landscape that surrounds Kangding b) Embark on the 12-hour bus ride back to Kangding.

Day 19: Head back to Chengdu for a well deserved early night. Days 20 - 22: Hop onto a bus bound for **Emei Shan** and spend two days hiking around this holy mountain.

Day 22: Take the short bus ride from Emei Shan to **Leshan** and spend the afternoon visiting the Giant Buddha before returning to Chengdu.

Day 23: Hang out in People's Park and pay a visit to the Yongling Tomb. If you're feeling brave, try the Sichuan spicy hot pot in the evening!

Days 24-25: Head out to **Qingcheng Shan** and spend two days visiting the mountain's temples and the **Dujiangyan Irrigation Project**, a marvellous ancient feat of engineering. Return to Chengdu in the evening.

Day 26: Visit the **Panda Breeding Research Centre** just outside of Chengdu where red pandas and giant pandas while away their lazy days. Appreciate the extreme efforts being made by the government to save these amazing species.

Day 27 - 29: Head down to Yibin and onto the **South Sichuan Bamboo Sea.** Spend a day and a half unwinding amongst the swaying mass of bamboo, hidden Buddhist shrines and flowing waterfalls. Make your back to Chengdu in the afternoon.

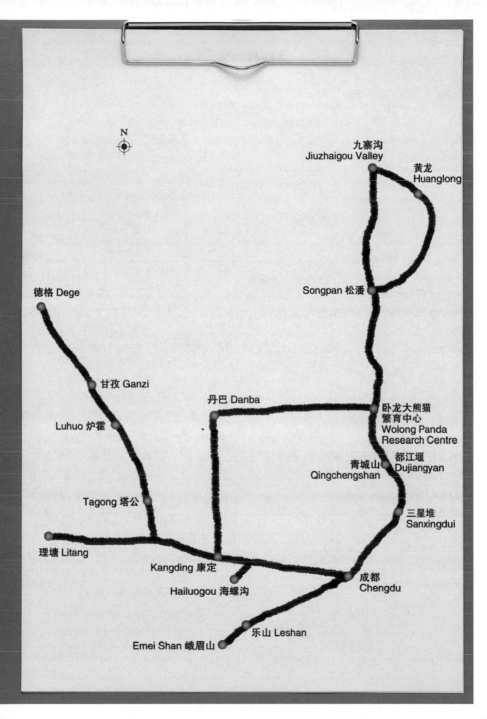

N

九寨沟
Jiuzhaigou Valley

黄龙
Huanglong

Songpan 松潘

德格 Dege

甘孜 Ganzi

Luhuo 炉霍

丹巴 Danba

卧龙大熊猫
繁育中心
Wolong Panda
Research Centre

青城山
Qingchengshan

都江堰
Dujiangyan

三星堆
Sanxingdui

Tagong 塔公

理塘 Litang

Kangding 康定

Hailuogou 海螺沟

成都
Chengdu

乐山 Leshan

Emei Shan 峨眉山

Index

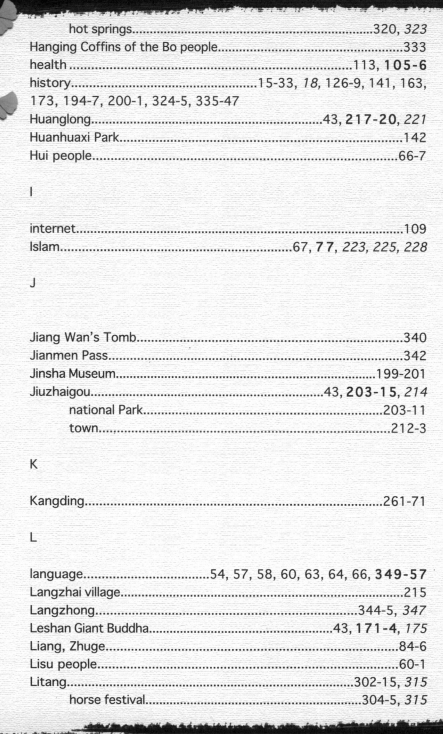

Q

R

S

T

China Through the Looking Glass, Sichuan

Managing Editor 主编：

 Zhang Gu（张谷）

Editors 编委：

 Chen Jialin (陈加林)

 Chen Xianchun（陈献春）

 Wu Mian（吴勉）

 Liu Meng（刘萌）

 Zhou Lunbin（周伦斌）

www.cnlookingglass.com

Chief Editor 策划：

 Quan Xinying (权新颖)

Authors 作家：

 Samantha Wilson

 Scott Lewis

Copy Editors 校审：

 Sarah Trott

 Samantha Wilson

Photography 图片提供：

 四川省旅游局, Samantha Wilson, Scott Lewis, Ray Au，

 Monique Jansen, Beijing Matric

Designers：

 Consultant, Gao Zhongyu (高中羽)

 Designer, Zhu Feifei (朱菲菲)

Translator 翻译：

 Zhou Xiaohui (周小卉), Ming Jiang (明江)

Sponsor 主办：

 Tourism Administration of Sichuan Province

 （四川省旅游局）

Published by 承办：

 The International Writers Club（国际作家俱乐部）

 Matric International Publishing House (迈萃国际出版）